Through the Storm

By

Dovia Winkelmann

I dedicate this book to my Journey.

All the glory be to my Almighty God. I am thankful He has graciously allowed me the time on Earth to start and finish this book. It was a struggle deciding how much of my story to put onto paper, and it has taken me many years to gather up courage—but here I am. Alive and able to tell the events and struggles that took place while in foster care which I tried to block out of my memory so many years ago, as well as the life, and the struggles that followed. I can now share the things that I only talked to God about, and the promises I made to him in return for deliverance out of the dark spaces that hovered over my emotional, spiritual, and mental state for more years than I could keep count.

In the midst of writing my story, I was reminded of the many occasions when I thought my life was one big joke (and not the kind you would laugh at). I would tell myself, "One day I will write a book about the crazy things I have had to endure in this life." I would tell others about my pain. The pain I experienced bouncing from one foster home to another, while my mom was strung out on drugs and somewhere selling and/or giving her body away, I'm sure for little-to-nothing. I would write about the pain that came from never knowing who my father was because of her actions, as well as the siblings I would never meet. I would write about how the siblings I did meet were just as broken as I was (maybe more), and how the brokenness resulted in us being unable to maintain any type of a healthy relationship. I would tell others how my need for love from a mother and father figure would eventually leave me bitter, depressed, destroyed, and constantly seeking love (or what I thought was love) in all the wrong places. I would tell others about my cries out to God throughout my past asking Him, 'why me?' and never stopping to think, 'why not me?' and how that affected me to the point that I became more and more consumed by the pain and sadness that seemed to always stay with

me.

The thought of writing a book would fade in and out my

mind over the years, but never completely go away. The

question "what if my struggles could one day help

another person?" always remained in a hidden place in

my mind.

In this book, I reflect and release those memories. I write

my story in the hope (like so many others) that by

sharing, I could help to break the cycle of broken homes,

broken children, and broken foster and biological parents.

I can only pray that others will continue to share their

stories, whatever they may be, so those in similar

situations know they are not alone. My story is for anyone

who needs to hear it. I only hope it is a reminder that

seeking help is never a sign of weakness, but that of

strength. If someone would have told me as a child, or

even young adult, to go talk to someone about how I was feeling, maybe I would not have been embarrassed to seek help over the years and maybe things in my life could have been different. This is something that I will now never know. I, too, am one of many who were not granted the opportunity to get help when it was clearly needed early on in life, and because of this, my trauma would have me suffering for years, like so many others who struggle with severe depression and anxiety.

I share in the hope that anyone who struggles with insecurities, and/or mental health issues as a result of being in the foster care system knows they are not alone. I pray they find my story encouraging, and that hopefully, when they read it, it will push them to mend the broken pieces of their hearts, and, most importantly, promote forgiveness. I do not know a single person who has lived a purpose-filled life who hasn't first been able to forgive those that hurt them. I know this because I, too, was unable to walk fully in my God-given purpose until I forgave those who hurt me.

I pray my story will fuel the souls of others to share their struggles (past and present), and encourage them to write that book, start that company, and just know that pain has no time limit. Only they will know when they are ready to let it go. When that time comes, take the pain and healing, and use it to help others. Let those struggling know there is a rainbow at the end of the storm if they just hang in there and never give up.

I write this book from a place of love, pain, anger, and an overall eagerness to share how God can and will bring you through all stages of life if you trust in Him and never give up. Know that God will never put more on you than you can bear. When you feel as though you can't take another step, I am a witness that if you continue to call out the name of God, He will come and direct your path.

If the journey you are on continuously leads you to one dead end after another, don't be afraid to switch paths. In this life, you may come to several dead ends before the right path is found, and that is okay. God sees and hears all and will always put you back on the right path. Those tears you cry, and your desperate calls for help are not going unheard. The Bible tells us that the eyes of the Lord are on the righteous and His ears hear our prayers. I believe the Bible is telling us that God is always here for us and listening. If we speak to Him and listen with an open heart, we will have the happiness we desire in this lifetime and the next.

It took a long time for me to realize that being in foster care didn't have to define who I was, or who I could become, and that my experiences didn't have to continue to have a negative impact on my future.

As children, we don't have a choice in the situations that we are placed in, but as adults, we are the authors of how our story will read if we stop allowing our past to haunt our present in negative ways. A bible verse God led me to as I started writing reads…

"I waited patiently for the Lord, and he inclined unto me, and heard my cry. He brought me up also out of a horrible pit, out of the miry clay, and set my feet upon a rock, and established my goings. And he hath put a new song in my mouth, even praise unto our God. Many shall see it, and fear, and shall trust in the Lord." [King James Version]

The Beginning

I have heard that your brain rarely remembers the events that happened in your life before the age of five. I'm not sure if this is true, but if so, I must be an exception to the rule. I am in my late 30s, and I remember events from the age of five and even a little before as if they happened yesterday. I remember a particular sunny day in 1986 vividly. It is the trauma from this day (and many other days to come) that would shape me to become the person I am today. This beautiful sunny day would be the start of a downward spiral of depression, abandonment issues, and suicidal thoughts and acts that would last for the next twenty-five years of my life. Have you ever heard someone say, "this feels like hell on earth"? Well, my hell was being a foster child—a continuous longing and wanting for someone and something to call my own, knowing it would never come. My hell was that feeling of loneliness and nothingness that slowly consumed my mind, body, and soul, day after day after day that I spent in foster care. My hell was carrying around my baggage with not a soul in sight to tell or show me how to lighten my load. I would carry my hell around with me for many years, until I finally figured out that I was my own hell, and if I wanted things to change in my life, it had to start within me. I learned that healing would ultimately be impossible to do alone. I would have to lean on a higher power to get me out of what had become my personal jail cell within myself.

Now, at this point you may be wondering where I am going with this, or maybe you're just confused. Heck, you may even be following all of it, but let me slow my thoughts down (like I frequently have to do) and start my story from the very beginning.

Aunt Wanda

Decatur, Illinois is the place I call home. Even though it never really felt like a home to me, it is where everything in my life would begin.

With the pain that I associate with this city, if the whole place sank into the Sangamon River, it wouldn't be missed by me.

Greenwood Circle, along with its many memories, would be the first neighborhood I can recall living in, but definitely not the last place I would live.

"Let's go, sis," Starsky screamed as he ran out the front door of our Aunt Wanda's house. Starsky was my older brother by four years. I was five years old at the time, and he was nine.

"Boy, slow down and wait for Via," Wanda yelled while rushing to her car heading to work. Aunt Wanda worked at one of the largest manufacturing plants in the area and was off to complete one of the many 12 to 16 hour shifts she often worked. She worked so much it was hard to tell if she was coming or going most days. With her being gone as much as she was, I'm not sure why she ever decided to take in two children that weren't biologically hers while her sister (my mother) chose to be in the streets. I would hear Aunt Wanda talking to other people about my mom bouncing between Decatur and Springfield, Illinois, which was about 30 minutes down the highway. It was said she was moving from place to place for drugs and going from man to man, as well as in and out of jail.

I guess Wanda felt it was her obligation as family to try and keep us out of the system and together as long as possible, so she did what she could.

Wanda was a petite-framed woman standing no taller than 5 feet tall, if that. She had a gorgeous brown complexion that carried not one scar or imperfection. Her skin was definitely a gift from God himself because she always looked way younger than her actual age. Most people were surprised to hear Wanda's age because the look of youth was definitely her friend for many years. I'm not sure if it was just genetics or the fact that she never sat still for long that kept her looking young and vibrant, but most could only wish to age as well.

"Wait, Starsky," I was now screaming, since Aunt Wanda was in her car, but he was already across the street and into the grassy area that led into the park. The park being within feet of Aunt Wanda's house meant many days and dark nights were spent swinging, sliding, running, and just enjoying being kids. Aunt Wanda's house was located on the edge of a large cul-de-sac, and

Greenwood Park was located right smack in the middle of it all. The cul-de-sac contained many homes and Aunt Wanda's home sat closest to the only entrance and exit in and out of the neighborhood. Greenwood Park was surrounded by homes, a large church, and an even larger cemetery. As a child I remember thinking how weird it was seeing people walking up and down the steps of that large church as they entered and exited Sunday morning, and immediately being surrounded by death. The iron gate across the street standing tall, serving as the entrance into the cemetery, instantaneously grabbed your attention. The headstones lined one after another behind it seemed to glare back at you, were always unnerving to me. I think back on it a lot and wonder if this was the devil's funny way of showing me what was to come, or maybe God's way of preparing me for life and death. Either way, at an early age, those headstones were embedded into my young brain and thoughts of death would begin to encompass my every thought.

Church would tell me, over and over again, scripture after scripture, not to fear death, and how if I lived my life the way God wanted of me, when the time came for my body to lay in the ground, just as so many others before me, my soul would go to Heaven to live on for eternity, and I would have eternal rest. Now imagine being a five-year-old concerned about dying, and then carrying that into your 30s. If this sounds terrible to you, then you can almost imagine how it felt living my life day after day, constantly worried about when death was coming for me. This, however, has been my life for as long as I can remember. In the years that followed, I came to the realization that the church and the grave were the Devil and God's way of speaking to me. They both seemed to be sitting on my shoulders talking to me. Sometimes at the same time and other times separately, trying to convince me of which path to go down. Let's just say throughout my life there were times when I listened to both voices, good and bad.

"I'm thirsty, Starsky," I yelled while running back across the grassy area and across the street to the house. We had been playing for so long that I was tired and in need of something to drink.

As I approached the front door of the house, I noticed it was pitch black inside. I turned the doorknob that led directly into the living room, and slowly walked inside. Immediately, a female voice yelled, "Get up."

Afraid, I stood still.

"It's just Via," said another voice from the other side of the room, sounding relieved. Via (short for Dovia) was the nickname given to me by one of Aunt Wanda's three daughters and that's what everyone called me. As I flipped the light switch on, two of my older cousins had *boys straddled on separate couches while their best friend Lisa was straddling a boy on the loveseat.*

"Cut the light off, Via, and watch out for Momma," another voice said.

I closed the open front door and did as I was told. I curled up in the corner of the love seat on the opposite end from where Lisa was straddling and laughing with a boy. I watched them until she gave me a look that I took to mean, "get back to work." Still curious as to what was going on around me, I split my time, half gazing out the window and the other half watching them grind and pants burn in Aunt Wanda's living room. (For those that haven't heard of pants burning, it's what people called making out while fully clothed back in the day). The pants burning session must have been way more exciting than looking out the window because I had missed Auntie's car pulling into the driveway.

"Run," someone screamed as keys could be heard jiggling around at the lock. Immediately bodies started to scatter everywhere. I curled up in the corner of the loveseat, scared, not knowing what was to come.

"What in the hell," Wanda screamed coming through the front door. Boys were already running from the living room, through the kitchen and out the back door before Wanda even had a chance to flip the light switch up.

Her backyard was surrounded by a fence so I can only imagine boys leaping over it trying to escape her wrath, not even taking the time to unlatch the gate. I couldn't blame them because I was young and still knew Auntie wasn't one to be messed with. Auntie Wanda was someone that you didn't want to upset. She became a different person when you made her mad, and not in a good way.

Lisa tried moving swiftly past Aunt Wanda, hoping to go unseen, but to no avail.

"Heffa, I see you, and will be calling your mom." Lisa knew better than to respond, so instead she kept her mouth closed and head down as she continued out the front door. Those were the last words stated before Aunt Wanda took her belt off and started going upside her daughters' heads and bodies. I started crying once the screaming began, watching Auntie whoop her teenage daughters. I knew not to utter a word as my body sank deeper into the loveseat. She had never struck me before and I didn't plan on it starting now.

This would be my first exposure, but definitely not my last, to what I found out was a good ol' fashioned butt whooping.

"Can't even enjoy a break from work without y'all getting into something," Wanda yelled while fixing her clothes and heading back out the front door. She headed back to work as if nothing had happened. One thing Wanda never allowed was anything or anyone to come in the way of her and money, and I mean nothing.

"Get up and get my house clean," Wanda screamed at the girls the next morning.

"I wasn't even here last night," Shelly the oldest said under her breath.

"What you say?"

"Nothing!" Shelly muttered.

"My house better be clean when I get off work, I know that." Auntie was headed back out the front door and off *to work once again. After the butt whoopings handed out the night before, you would think the house would get clean and all would be quiet today, but nope! They acted unphased, as if Wanda going upside their heads and bodies with belts the prior night was nothing new.*

"Let's have a card party," Tiffany said with no hesitation. Tiffany was the no-fear sister of the three. She did what she wanted and worried about the consequences later. Immediately, an argument ensued amongst the sisters over whether or not to have friends over to play cards. Clarissa (the sister clearly against the festivities) lost the argument, because before you knew it the sun had gone down and drinks were flowing. Tunk and Deuces was being played at the round table in Wanda's kitchen. I'm pretty sure no one was of legal age to drink, but that didn't stop them. Lisa walked in the front door with a young boy following close behind. He looked to be about my age, and I remember him to this day for a couple

different reasons. One, his head was bigger than any child I had ever seen before, and two, he wore the biggest smile on his face. He had a smile that I'm sure was complimented daily by adults he encountered.

"Via, this my little brother Brandon, take him and y'all go and play." Brandon and Lisa had to be over a decade apart in age. When Lisa's mom had to work, or just had something to do, Lisa was put in charge of watching Brandon. Lisa didn't seem to mind, as it was pretty normal in the 80s that older siblings or relatives acted as if they were the parent while the actual parent or guardian was out God-knows-where doing who-knows-what.

"Girl, did you get in trouble last night?" Clarissa asked Lisa as she headed to the table.

"Naw, I don't even think your momma called mine, but even if she did you know my momma ain't never home." Everyone laughed at Lisa as she headed to take her seat at the table. Once the boys from the night before had arrived, quarters and dollars were being thrown into the center of the table, and the gambling had begun.

Brandon decided we should play hide and seek, so I agreed. Starsky, who was standing close by not saying much, decided he wanted to play as well. We went to hide as Brandon started counting. We took turns counting and hiding until it was Brandon's turn to seek again.

He whispered in my ear to go and hide in my bedroom closet. Even at five years old, the way that he said it let me know that he didn't want to just play hide and seek anymore. He started counting as I went to hide. I did as he told me and opened the mirrored closeted door and crawled inside. I pulled the door closed behind me and slid on top of the shoes thrown about. Brandon yelled,

"20," loudly from the other room, probably so Starsky would stay in hiding while he set out to "seek" us.

I heard him approaching as he slowly slid the door open. Once he saw I had listened and was inside, that huge smile spread across his face once again.

"Lay down," he whispered as he got inside. I did as I was told and went from a sitting position to an uncomfortable lying position on top of the shoes. Brandon crawled in closer and laid on top of me. We lay still for what felt like an eternity saying and doing nothing. I started to replay the night before and remembered seeing my cousins and Lisa moving their hips back and forth with their guys. Not knowing what else to do, I attempted moving mine back and forth. Brandon smiled again while leaning in close attempting to kiss my lips. I immediately turned my head. Even at a young age, something about kissing didn't seem like something you just did. Kissing seemed *special, not like the pants burning we were currently doing.*

"It's cool," Brandon responded at my head turn. I don't think he even cared about kissing, he was probably just attempting to do what he had seen someone older doing, just like I was. "Pull your pants down," Brandon whispered. Was he crazy? First, he tried kissing me, and now he wanted me to take my pants off. As I lay uncomfortable in the tight space considering it, his smile widened, if that was possible. I jiggled at my pants button, wanting to say no, but something else in me wanting to say, "okay."

I hadn't a chance to say either before we were snapped back to reality. We were kids playing adult games but play time was coming to a screeching halt. Aunt Wanda's voice could be heard echoing throughout the closet. She must have been off from work or on a break, but it was definitely her voice.

"What y'all got going on in here?" I heard Auntie voice say walking through the front door. It didn't sound as if she was angry, but I had seen what happened the night before, and knew what was to come next.

"Get out, Get out." Brandon jumped off me and out of the closet. Afraid, I immediately hurried and slid the door shut behind him. I once again was surrounded by nothing but darkness, afraid to move. I had seen what happened to people that pissed Wanda off, and I wanted no part of that. I had been stupid, and at any moment the screaming and beatings would begin. I could only pray they didn't come my way. The longer I lay, the more nothing happened, and the more confused I became. I slowly eased the door open and peeked out to see if I could see Wanda coming my direction. When I didn't see her but heard laughing instead, I eased further out the closet and then out my bedroom door.

I walked down the short hallway that led to the kitchen. Starsky had come out of hiding and was standing there next to Brandon watching the card game. Everyone was sitting and laughing, appearing to have a good time as money continued to be thrown around.

Once Aunt Wanda saw me peeking around the corner, she waved me to come over. I was sure that this was it and she knew what I had been up to. I got closer expecting to be hit, but to my surprise, instead of screaming and beatings like I had been waiting for since she arrived, she looked at me and smiled.

"You hungry, Via?"

"Yes!" I responded quickly, glad she was asking me this, and nothing else.

"Y'all been here all day and haven't fed these kids? Shelly, get that chicken out the fridge and fry it up."

Before too long the house smelled of fried chicken, and happiness was in the air all around.

From the outside looking in, this would appear to be a good night, but unfortunately, later in life, I would discover that this was one of many nights that would include Wanda sitting around a table, gambling. She sometimes even traveled to the nearest large city, like St. Louis, in hopes of winning it big. You always knew if she was a winner or loser that night by her attitude when she got back home. I would replay this night over and over again in my head in the years that followed.

When I would replay the night, I continuously came to the same conclusion. Auntie was only happy that night because there was money to be won. Beatings weren't handed out that night because Wanda had a need and it was being met. If you had money, you better hold on tight to it when she was around. You never knew when she was ready to feed her addiction with something that belonged to you. Neither age nor relation mattered when money was involved.

Here I go again with my fast-moving thoughts, once again jumping ahead. Just trust me when I say: stay with me, this is just the beginning.

Day from Hell

This is the day I call the day from hell. It is that sunny day in 1986 that I remember so vividly. I woke up like I did most days with the sun beaming into my room over my bunk bed. I just loved that wooden bed. I loved the fact that most nights I had the whole thing to myself, and I could choose to sleep on the bottom or the top. Most of the time I chose to sleep up top because it gave me the feeling of being on top of the world. When I was up there, nothing else mattered, and it brought me so much happiness. Even the permanent scar that I carry with me below my chin from falling off the top bunk never deterred me from climbing right back up there again and again.

That morning, I could hear voices coming from the front of the house, so I decided to throw on some clothes and see what was going on. I walked out of my room and down the hallway into the living room immediately noticing that things didn't look right. Heads were down and the happiness that once occupied the space was now gone, replaced with sadness. I assumed that maybe someone had passed away and needed to be buried in that cemetery across the way, but I wasn't sure. Shelly was walking away from me crying, and Aunt Wanda continued to move from the kitchen to the living room appearing to clean the house.

"Momma, don't do this," Tiffany said out loud, but Aunt Wanda continued moving, not even acknowledging what was just said. Once she was back to the living room and seated on the couch, she began to wave her hand for us to come over. Starsky was up and dressed by this time as well and was standing in the living room beside me as Aunt Wanda began delivering news neither of us was ready for.

"Y'all can't live here. I work way too much and have no reliable help. I can't do this anymore."

I wasn't quite sure what that meant, so my little body stayed still, and my mouth stayed quiet as I listened. What did she mean by she can't do this anymore? What was "this"? My brain started going into overdrive. Tiffany cried out that she would do better, and help out more, as she walked to her bedroom with tears streaming down her face. She slammed her bedroom door and surprisingly Wanda said nothing. At that moment it was confirmed, something definitely wasn't right. What was going on? Wanda's expression never changed as she continued talking. She delivered the news as if what she was saying was no big deal. If it wasn't for everyone crying, it may have taken me longer to realize her news definitely wasn't good. I remember the sadness I felt at the sight of my cousins crying. While they cried nothing came from Wanda. Up to this point in my life I hadn't seen her cry about anything. She was always so strong.

Knocking on the front door was the next thing I remember. When Auntie stood to go answer it, an eerie feeling came over me that I will never forget. When the door opened back, my eyes laid sight on the most beautiful woman I had ever seen. Her face was small and round, and her petite frame complemented her whole appearance. She wore slacks with a blazer and blouse underneath. Her hair was rocking the cutest pixie cut, and her whole appearance reminded me of the actress Nia Long in her short hair days.

The lady standing in the door looked young and wore a genuine looking smile. Her skin had a glow that radiated from her brown complexion, or maybe it was just the bright sun. Either way, she was beautiful. Once Wanda stepped a little more to one side, I noticed that the lady wasn't alone. There was a white police officer standing there in uniform. He, too, wore a smile on his face that initially made me believe that everything was going to be okay. Aunt Wanda stepped out of the way inviting the two to come in.

"Hi, my name is Joyce," she said, introducing herself to Starsky and I as she entered. Joyce took her seat on the edge of the couch while the officer stood close by the door choosing not to sit. "Come have a seat," Joyce patted the cushion next to her.

For some reason everybody kept trying to get us to sit down, and it wasn't registering to me yet why. Furthermore, what did Auntie mean when she said we couldn't live in our home anymore? Those words started to repeat themselves over and over in my brain. As Joyce began to talk to us, Aunt Wanda's house phone began to ring. She excused herself to go and answer it while Joyce *was saying something about being our caseworker (whatever that meant). While Joyce continued talking, Aunt Wanda attempted to speak low in a tone so as not to be overheard. I could hear bits and pieces of what she was telling the person on the other end. "You better not come here." "The police here." "These not my kids, don't tell me what I shouldn't do." Once Auntie realized she was raising her voice and the officer was looking her way, she quickly hung up the phone. Wanda's facial expression immediately went from one of anger, to one prepared to force a smile once again for the guests in her home.*

"Starsky and Dovia, you guys have to come with me, Joyce said." She was no longer sitting on the edge of the couch, smiling, but had risen to a standing position. "I have homes for you to live in."

As mature as I may have been for 5 years old, my mind couldn't comprehend any of what this caseworker lady was saying. That beautiful face that entered the house moments earlier was now becoming ugly, it too etched into my little brain to forever stay. Sometime between the night before and today Aunt Wanda had thrown some of Starsky's and my clothes into trash bags, and now had them sitting by the kitchen. Was she throwing her trash out or us? Had she nibbled off her plate all she could and now she was finished? Done! Starsky and I had now become trash that was headed to the dump. Did I hear her right? Did she say homes? She wasn't even taking us to the same dump so that we could at least be together? Joyce started walking to the door as the officer grabbed the trash bags of clothes. Crazily enough, we weren't even taken out the front door that they had come in. I was taken kicking and screaming out the same back door that the boys had fled over prior. Starsky had no reaction and did as he was told without a fight.

"Auntie, please, no! No! No!" I screamed. Even though I didn't know what I had done, I yelled over and over how sorry I was. I didn't know why I was sorry, but I was willing to not do whatever it was again. I continued kicking and screaming as Joyce held on even tighter to me.

The officer opened the back gate and looked around before walking out to open the door to the car that had been parked out on the back street. Joyce put me in the open door, while Starsky followed. The officer and Joyce had come in two separate cars so once we were in her car along with our trash bags, he walked to his police car and got inside and waited.

"Via, Via," I heard someone screaming as Joyce was trying to get me calm in the backseat. Clarissa, the youngest of Wanda's girls, was now standing in the back

screen door screaming out my name. Clarissa had become my favorite of the three daughters because she spent the most time with me, dressing me up in the cutest clothes and taking me to the nearby store for treats. She always let me tag along with her and never once acted as if I was a bother. I hadn't seen her at all this morning until now. It was too late though. We were off to the dump. Joyce tried to console us saying everything would be okay, but I just looked out the back window and screamed more. Brandon had lied saying everything was okay, and now Joyce was starting in with her lies. Everyone said, "it will be okay," but did they really know? I am sure that this is the day that all my trust issues would begin with not only men, but family and people in general. Everyone I knew lied to me, and I believed no one could be trusted. As Joyce settled into the driver's seat, the day seemed to stand still. It was a sunny day, but all my eyes could see was darkness. The beauty that the sun brought into my bedroom window just

that morning was now gone.

My eyes drifted from the car window to the sidewalk.

There stood a dark-skinned woman who grabbed my

attention. She stood looking at me, not moving or saying

a word. Had this woman seen me kicking and screaming

to the car? Was she a stranger that was saddened by

what she was seeing? Her face looked so sad. Had she

stood by and watched the whole thing? What was it

about her face that brought such familiarity? Who was

she? I was no longer crying for me; I was watching her.

She didn't carry the beauty Joyce did. Her face looked

worn and tired. She carried around the face of someone

that had been through a lot. I didn't know why, but I

became even more saddened at the sight of her. The

tears started to flow harder now as I screamed even

louder for Aunt Wanda to not let this happen. My tears

changed nothing as Joyce slowly pulled away from the stranger on the sidewalk and Greenwood, forever.

What started as just another beautiful sunny day would become the reason it would be hard to ever consider any place my home again. The only home I had known pushed me and my brother out on the street and stayed rooted right where it was. I, on the other hand, would be uprooted time after time again in the years to come. I never stayed in one place long enough for it to ever feel like a home. Home was a fairytale and real life was about to hit me harder than I could ever imagine. Who could have known that what started out as just another sunny day would start a nightmare that was not a dream but my reality? On this day began the real journey that lay ahead for me.

Life Changer

By the time I had reached the age of 9, life hadn't been terrible, but it hadn't been good either. I had bounced around to more than a few foster homes, and even more church homes. It seemed like every foster home I lived in was either a believer of God, or just enjoyed the fashion show that Sunday morning brought into the church. Life was beginning to force me to grow up way before my time.

Figuring out who to trust and who not to trust had become routine. To make it easy for myself I chose to trust no one. I had heard the words, "you will be okay," more times than I could keep count by then and had grown tired of hearing it. The reality was that I was not okay, and I hated people who pretended as if they understood what I was going through. They hadn't the slightest idea what it felt like bouncing around from home *to home. They didn't know what it felt like to never have a mom or dad in their life. They did not know what it felt like to not know how to love, the same way I didn't know what it felt like to be loved. People assume that foster care means that a child has been removed from a place where their needs were not being met, and now they were being met. That a child has been removed from one unsafe environment and moved to a safe one. Heck no! For me, it was hoping that the next home wasn't just out for the little check that came along with taking in a foster kid. Up to this point, Joyce had been the most consistent person in my life, and I battled with myself often how I felt about her. I never knew if she was just stopping by to visit or relocating me yet once again. On her last visit to see me she had spoken to me about how she was working to reunite me and Starsky together in the same home. I was happy about this possibility, because even though I was younger, I felt like I could better look out for him if we were together. Starsky was what people called retarded in the 80s. It made me so angry but also sad every time I heard people say it because he wasn't. He was just like everyone else, it just took him longer to learn things, and some things he just couldn't learn. He struggled with reading and writing, but who doesn't struggle with something? I never looked at him or talked to him any differently, because in my eyes, he wasn't. As a child who had no control over the thoughts and actions of others, I was limited in what I could do or say, but always felt like he needed me there to protect him when people were mean for no reason. Us being in the same home would definitely help because I had his back.*

Joyce had followed through on her promise and this was the day that Starsky and I would join together in the same foster home after being separated for four long years. This next home would become what would become my biggest life changer yet.

We traveled to the new house with wonder filling my mind. The new journey that came with every move still excited me up to this point. I knew I wasn't going back to Wanda so I tried my best to imagine what the new foster home would be like. As Joyce drove, I sat there wondering what possibilities were to come for us. Would this foster home be nice and want to adopt us? Would there be other kids living there as well? Would the new place include a foster mom and dad, or just one or the other? I had so many questions inside my head with no answers. Joyce didn't tell me anything about the new home so whatever was to come would definitely be a surprise.

Once she had parked the car, we walked the sidewalk that led up to a two-family duplex. Instead of joy, that feeling of uneasiness once again came over me just as it had the day Wanda opened her front door four years prior.

As we started to climb the few stairs leading to the front porch, I became even more uncertain of what was to come. Starsky looked at me as though he was just as unsure as I was, and Joyce looked at the both of us as if she needed to assure us with a smile that all was well. She began knocking on the front door while I stood beside her not knowing what to expect on the other side. Once Joyce knocked a second time, the lady living in the adjacent apartment opened her door. When she saw the visitors knocking weren't for her, she gave a nod and quickly closed her door. The door Joyce had been knocking on suddenly opened and an older woman appeared behind the screened door. She gave us a smile as she unlocked and opened it for us to enter. Even as a child, I remember that smile bringing no peace to my young mind. The way the corners of her mouth curled up made it appear forced.

She had a face that looked old from years of living but carried no wrinkles. Her skin color resembled mine, very dark in color. I had been called "blacky" a lot because of my complexion and wondered if as a child she had been too. She looked to be in her 60s standing at least six feet tall with a built, but not large frame. The defined tone in her arms and legs surprised me for someone of her age because she had no flab. Her hair was an off black color that had several strips of gray throughout. She wore a curl in it that appeared to be formed from a hot comb and rollers. It looked as if she may have had it freshly done in preparation for our arrival. She opened the screen door back even more and welcomed us all to come inside. Once inside her apartment, I noticed it was clean and everything seemed to have a place. Things in it appeared old including the awful looking carpet covering her living room floor, and the older looking furniture she had placed throughout the room, perfected, I'm sure, just how she wanted it. The living room, being the first room you entered coming through the front door, contained a large brown recliner with a matching brown couch and loveseat. Alongside the recliner and couch were older-looking, dark, wooden end tables. I gave Joyce a look to tell her this wasn't the home for us, and to try again. I knew foster parents weren't lining up in droves to take in kids, but something didn't feel right about this home. Joyce clearly didn't understand my look because once the bags were inside, she gave Starsky and I glances and said, "you will be fine here, I promise." Promises were once again being made without the slightest idea if everything was actually going to be okay. Joyce shared a few more words and smiles with our new foster mom and us, and then just like that she was gone.

Our new foster mom told us to call her Mrs. Rice, and over the next five long years of our stay with her, we wouldn't learn much more about Mrs. Rice than what we knew the day we moved in. It would be quite a while *before I even knew her first name as something other than Mrs., and that didn't happen by her telling me.*

The longer we lived with her, we happened to hear and see things. I once overheard the landlord of the two-family apartment call Mrs. Rice by her first name as he collected the rent money. That was my exposure to learning a little more about the lady we now lived with. Even then, knowing her name, I knew better than to ever disrespect her by saying it out loud. She didn't take much, especially disrespect. She was very old-school in every aspect.

Mrs. Rice never talked much about her life which always made me wonder, did her mom not want her? Did she not know her dad, like me? Did she have a bad childhood? Why did she always look so unhappy, and why didn't she have friends that she talked to regularly on the phone, or visited with? Mrs. Rice didn't have any children that we knew of, and no one really came to check on her. There were no pictures of family or loved ones displayed anywhere around her home. She was simply a mystery to me. Joyce had kept her promise of reunification of Starsky and me, but whether it would be worth what we would endure over the next five years would turn out to be the real question.

"You bet not cry," Mrs. Rice said as she slapped me upside my head. I was in a chair, on my knees, bent over the sink, holding on for dear life to a towel draped around me. Mrs. Rice had placed it around my neck to catch any water that may fall during the washing process. Getting my hair washed and pressed was my worst nightmare, times two. The shampoo always seemed to burn my eyes causing me to cry and scream out in pain every time, and every time I cried, Mrs. Rice would hit me across my head causing me to scream even louder. After the wash, braid up, and overnight dry of day one came day two, *which included the pressing comb. The preparation that led up to the hair pressing was the worst. I could never sleep the night before, and always felt as if I was preparing for my own funeral.*

I would have to line the floor around the sink and oven with newspaper to catch any hair that might fall as I sat on a little wooden stool waiting for the hot comb to be applied. Watching her set the hot comb to the bare flame to heat up, and then taking it off to be applied to my dry coarse hair always made my anxiety peak and stress levels go up. There was no amount of time that ever got me used to the pain of the heat burning my ears, neck, and forehead over and over again. The smell of burning hair forever stays with me, as well as the unexpected blows upside the head that came when I was unable to sit still and take the pain. Once the wash and press was finished, I was able to semi-relax as my scalp was oiled with Sulfur 8 oil that reeked of death. The quick relief from the anxiety that I had during the pressing process would quickly turn into anger once she began putting my hair in the same 4 ponytails that I despised dearly. This time in particular, they were despised even more. Mrs. Rice had decided to braid each ponytail to the very end and attach barrettes. I had to be the only 9-year-old in all of Decatur walking around with kiddie ponytails and barrettes. Mrs. Rice was so old that either she didn't realize it or just didn't care that this style wasn't in style.

The next day was picture day and I refused to take pictures in ponytails and barrettes. I had come up with a plan, and my next move would be to figure out the execution of it. I finally decided I would take down the ponytails before I went to the bus stop that next morning. I would then put them back in before I got back to the house that afternoon. Mrs. Rice would never have to even know what I had done. I knew she wouldn't be purchasing school pictures because I didn't plan on telling her about them. There was no reason I could think of as to why my plan shouldn't work.

The next morning as Mrs. Rice laid in bed, I put my plan into action. Our clothes had been laid out the night before so there was no need for her to get up and out of bed. I put on my light color stone washed overalls, a cute top and was ready to go. I peeked to make sure Mrs. Rice was still in bed, then went to the furthest part of the apartment where my room was and took my ponytails out. I brushed and combed my hair the best I could before calling out to Mrs. Rice that I was leaving. Without waiting for a response, I eased out the backdoor and down the street. I prayed she hadn't gotten up and made her way to the front door as she sometimes did. I ran as fast as I could to the bus stop, hoping not to hear her calling out to me. Luckily for me, I heard nothing.

I stood with pride as one of the girls at the bus stop looked in amazement at what I can only assume was the length and the waviness of my hair. It could have just been a confused look because I was no longer rocking my regular ponytails, but whatever, she was still looking at me, and I knew it. As the bus pulled to my stop, I walked on and took my seat with all the confidence in the world. All eyes were on me. I smiled knowing my plan was in effect and working. As the bus drove to school sharp shooting pains began to take over my stomach. I wasn't sure what was coming but felt like the pain I was experiencing had to be a sign that whatever was to come was not going to be good. I prayed my sixth sense of feeling things happening before they actually did was not correct this time, and I was just worrying myself for no reason about Mrs. Rice catching me.

Becoming a Woman

As the time approached for our class to go and take pictures, the sharp shooting pains intensified, only now they moved not only through my stomach but my back as well. Was I worrying myself into sickness for no reason, or was something worse about to happen? When it was time to go stand and take pictures my body wouldn't allow me to move. I was frozen in my seat.

Tears had begun to flow as my teacher rushed over to see what the commotion was surrounding my desk. I tried fighting the tears back out of embarrassment, but the pain had become unbearable. My teacher looked down at me and told me I would be okay before rushing back to her desk to make a call.

"I need assistance with taking my class to take pictures," she said. "I have an emergency."

I was once again being told I was okay, but I wasn't sure she knew what she was talking about either because I felt like I was dying. I had decided if death was coming that would be okay with me, I just didn't want the pain that was coming with it. Once her assistance had arrived, and had taken the class for pictures, my fourth-grade teacher informed me that it looked as if I had started my period.

"My what," I thought, unable to speak due to the pain.

I was assisted with standing to my feet and getting to the nurse's office before my teacher departed.

My pants were now ruined and completely covered in blood. Not understanding what was going on with my body only confirmed that the blood meant death, and it was coming sooner than later.

The nurse then delivered news to me that was far worse than the pain, blood, or the fact that I wasn't actually dying. She said the words that I never wanted to hear.

"I have to call your mom," the nurse stated, picking up the receiver.

"No!!!!" I pleaded through the pain. I knew she meant Mrs. Rice and instantly I became terrified of what would happen when she saw my hair, forget the blood!

"I have to sweetie, she has to come get you, and take you home," the nurse said softly.

The nurse called Mrs. Rice to explain that my menstrual cycle had begun, and I would need to be picked up. The nurse didn't know, but she had just been the delivery person of my death sentence, and I would never have the courage to tell her. Within 30 minutes, Mrs. Rice was standing in the nurse's station looking down at me as I lay on the loveseat. My heart felt as if it would jump out of my chest once our eyes locked and I connected with her glare. I had attempted to gather my hair back in ponytails as I laid and waited, but the look on her face said I had failed drastically. The look she gave me was one of either shock, anger, or both, but they all terrified me just the same. Mrs. Rice gave the nurse the same fake smile I had seen her give Joyce and other strangers so many times before, but it never fooled me. She thanked her for calling and turned to walk out of the office without saying as much as a word to me.

I followed at a slow pace behind her, finding it hard to walk on my own, let alone keep up with her long legs. Once I was seated in the backseat of the car, I noticed that Mrs. Rice was peering through the rearview mirror. I hadn't even attempted to sit up front because that would be too close for comfort. She looked at me for a while as *if she was trying to figure out what to say, or if she wanted to say anything at all.*

"So, you want to be grown?" I knew how I wanted to answer her question but knew it wouldn't be the response she wanted to hear, so I chose to be smart by keeping my head down and saying nothing at all. The closer we got to the house, the more nervous I became. I wondered if the pain in my stomach would outweigh the pain that was about to hit my butt. Once the car was parked, Mrs. Rice got out, again not uttering a word. All other times the car ride to the house seemed to take forever, but this day it felt like we made two turns and magically there we were. Having no choice, I got out of the backseat, making sure to stay as far behind her as I possibly could. I figured if she swung her fist, at least I would see it coming. She was different though once we were in the house. She looked as if she almost cared about how I was feeling for a brief moment.

"Go and wash up," she said, handing me a pad, clean underwear, and a rag to wash with.

She didn't say or explain anything about my period so thank goodness it was obvious what I needed to do with the items she had given me. I could hear her talking from the kitchen telling me all the things I couldn't do while on my period. I couldn't go swimming, take a bath, or even get my hair washed while on my period, was all I heard. Not being able to get my hair washed was the only positive thing coming from this whole experience. I guess this was what Mrs. Rice called "the talk," even though she hadn't really said much. I didn't understand why I wasn't supposed to do those things, and sure wasn't planning on asking for any explanations. I was still unsure as to why I was in such pain with so much blood coming out of me and still alive. I stood in the bathroom with tears once again flowing, cringing in pain.

"Come on out here and get this medicine and food," Mrs. Rice called out.

After eating the soup and taking the medicine I did as I was told and went to lay down. I tossed and turned for what felt like hours before the medicine finally kicked in and I was able to drift off to sleep.

"YOU GROWN, HUH," is all I heard as the strikes began.

Mrs. Rice was asking me the same question from earlier, only this time stating the answer, and not waiting for me to answer as she began hitting me.

The strikes from the broom handle struck me over and over again. The handle hit me with so much force that by the second or third hit, it had broken in half. I thought this would make her stop, but it didn't. It was as if she were in *a zone, and there was no stopping her. Mrs. Rice just continued beating me with the part of the broom that was still intact. The pain from the broom was so intense I screamed out in agony. Mrs. Rice responded to my shrieks by hitting harder the louder I cried.*

"Why?" I screamed, but she didn't answer, just kept beating.

Starsky must have come home from school while I was sleeping because out of the corner of my eye, I could see him peeking from around the corner of his bedroom. I tried to move away from the handle as I cried out in pain, but she stayed on me. She was keeping up with me as if she was going to prove her point and a lesson would be learned one way or another. There was no remorse on her face, just one strike after another, the next one harder than the one before. Once my body had taken all it could, my mind drifted off to another place, and for a brief moment the pain became easier to bear as she swung again and again. Once she was satisfied with her work, or thought a lesson was learned, she slid her house shoes back on her feet (which had come off while chasing me in circles) and told me to go clean myself up. I looked down at myself not knowing if the blood I was seeing was from me becoming a woman at nine, or from the new welts now engraved into my body. I closed the bathroom door and melted to the ground. I lay on the ground crying silently until I had no more tears left to cry. I then pulled myself up off the ground and looked in the mirror and asked God, "Why?" The only other thing I knew to do was pray.

"Take my life, God," I silently cried out. "I am super black, ugly, and she hates me, please just take my life," I said, begging to God and the bathroom mirror in front of me.

We went to church every Sunday with Mrs. Rice. The pastor preached about God hearing our pleas, but if this was so, why didn't he hear mine? This God could not exist, or he would never allow me to feel this type of pain. He would never allow this woman to beat me the way she did, especially over ponytails. I knew I shouldn't have taken them down, but did I deserve this type of pain over it? I stood looking in the mirror unintentionally justifying ponytails as the reason for the beating, instead of thinking there is never a reason to beat me.

That night started years of abuse to come, and the relationship that was formed between the mirror and me. I talked and cried to that mirror so much it became a friend to me. Beating after beating I would ask it, "Why me?"

"Get out the bathroom," Mrs. Rice yelled from the living room. I'm sure she was sitting in her big, tan reclining

chair with those huge peeling feet propped up. She would beat me and act as if it had taken so much out of her, like she was the one now needing her rest from a day of hard work. I didn't understand it then, and to this day, I still struggle with it. It seemed to me the smart thing to do would be to not beat me, but talk to me, and just maybe she wouldn't be exhausted. Mrs. Rice never discussed or gave any reasoning behind why she beat me. I guess in her mind there was no explanation that needed to be given to a child. That night I went to bed once again changed forever, but in a different way this time. I was now not only scorned, but a woman.

A Friend

The next couple of years in Mrs. Rice's home was nothing short of torture. She continued to beat me, and eventually started beating Starsky as well. I wasn't able to protect him, and he wasn't able to protect me. The older we got the meaner she became. I think we both just eventually grew used to knowing we were going to be beaten with extension cords, branches, shoes, belts, brooms, and whatever else she chose to use across our bodies on any given day. Even when I tried to make my mind drift away from the pain, the welts were always proof to remind me of what had happened. When we didn't cry, or at least cry loud enough, Mrs. Rice would only swing harder. There was no stopping her, and I knew it. On top of the beatings, I was developing this new body that nobody was taking the time to talk to me about. This made things even harder for me and the depression quickly started to take over more intensely than before, *only I didn't know what it was at the time that was making me feel so hopeless and sad.*

The time came in my life to begin a new journey called middle school. It was something that I definitely wasn't ready for. Entering middle school was hard for me. My skin color didn't magically become lighter like I had prayed it would on so many nights, and Mrs. Rice was still doing my hair minus the barrettes and treating me as if I meant nothing to her. The other students were going to laugh at me, and I knew it. The size of my nose and forehead had always been the focus of others' laughter, so I knew middle school would be no different. I thought if only I could just drop out or run away, things would be so much easier, but easy and my life never coincided.

The only thing that distracted the boys from my flaws was my figure. I never thought my body looked good until it became the topic of the boys' overheard conversations.

Apparently, my butt was the largest of any of the other middle school girls, and for whatever reason the boys seemed to love it. I hated feeling like that was all they were looking at, but I had convinced myself it was better than them making fun of me all the time.

"Come here, fivehead," Mike yelled down the hall at me, referring to my large forehead. His friends laughed, and so did I to hide my embarrassment.

"What do you want, boy?" I asked with a smile, trying not to look annoyed.

"You already know, quit playing." Mike hurt my feelings a lot, but because I had a crush on him, I took whatever attention he was willing to give, good or bad. At least he was giving me attention, I told myself. I backed up against my locker, allowing him to get close enough access to feel my butt. Once he had gotten his quick feel,

he moved on with his boys, laughing as if I never existed. I got my books out of my locker and continued down the hall, noticing a familiar looking face coming my direction. I had seen her a couple times before at Church, but we had never spoken.

"Hi, my name is Leah," she said, stopping in front of me to introduce herself. Girls weren't the nicest, so for her to stop and introduce herself was a shock. "Don't I know you?" she asked.

"I think we have seen each other before," I replied. Leah was definitely someone you would consider fly. Her hair was fixed in a cute ponytail with extensions, and she had on a pair of fitted jeans with matching top. Her shape made the pants she had on fit her figure to perfection. Leah had a little button nose, and a large forehead. Even though her forehead was large like mine, the boys didn't tease her the way they did me. When your skin was on *the lighter side like hers, people seemed more forgiving of noticeable flaws, or so it seemed in the 90s. There was even a saying that went something like "if you light then you alright." I wasn't so lucky to be blessed with the light skinned genes, so I was never "alright."*

"I think you live down the street from me," Leah said to me.

"I live on Union Street."

"So do I," she replied. "Cool, you walk home with me after school." She gave me a quick smile before turning and heading down the hallway to her next class.

The school bell rang at the end of the day, and just like Leah had said, she was waiting at the bottom of the school's entrance stairs.

"Come on," she said, waving me over. Without hesitation, I followed her. I assumed she wouldn't think any more about me after her initial introduction, but she hadn't forgotten me. I grew excited at the thought of having someone to talk to that not only wanted to talk to me, but was cute and sweet, and not conceited in any way from what I could tell.

Leah lived about a block away from Mrs. Rice's house. Her house came first so we stopped once we reached the gate out front. Something in my head told me to keep walking, but the moment Leah invited me inside her house, I couldn't say no. Her house wasn't like the duplex. She lived in a white large two-story single-family home. It was an older home, but larger than any home I had ever been in. There was nothing fancy about it, but it screamed family. There were bikes and balls thrown all about the front yard, which let me know Leah wasn't an only child. As we walked inside her house, there were people everywhere moving about the house.

"Who are all these people?" I whispered.

She immediately started laughing and said, "My brothers and sisters." Leah came from a large family of 8 siblings, 5 girls and 3 boys. "Come on, let's go upstairs."

Once we were in what appeared to be a shared bedroom, Leah tossed her school bag onto a bed.

"Come on out the bathroom, Davida," Deja yelled at the bathroom door.

"I'm doing my hair," the voice in the bathroom yelled back. Leah instantly got mad and began yelling for her sister to come out.

"You are always doing your hair, and you have a bedroom, I need to use the bathroom now." Leah's sister walked out of the bathroom looking irritated at her little sister. Even with her hair half done, she was beautiful. She was not only as cute as Leah, but maybe cuter. They both had the same button nose and features, but there was something about Davida's beauty that stood out. I must have been staring because the look of irritation was now focused on me. I instantly felt uneasy. I didn't want her to think I was crazy or weird, so I turned back to her and blurted out the first thing that came to mind.

"We have the same name."

"What?" she said with an attitude.

"Well, my name is Dovia, and yours is Davida so it's almost like the same name. That kinda makes us like sisters already." After I made the statement, I realized

how crazy I must have sounded, and was immediately

embarrassed. She looked at me for a second before

laughing. Once I saw her laughing, I relaxed and I too,

started laughing. As Leah came out of the bathroom a

male voice was yelling up the stairs.

"It's time for prayer, come on down," he said in a stern

and serious voice.

"My dad is home from work, you better go." I hadn't seen

their dad, but by the tone of his voice, and the way they

both headed to the stairs, I knew he was serious, and

they had better listen to him. As we headed downstairs to

the living room, the whole family was going to their knees

using couches and chairs as support. Not knowing what

was happening I moved swiftly to the front door.

"Come pray with us," Leah's dad insisted. Starsky and I

went to church every Sunday with Mrs. Rice, but I never

knew people prayed like this in their home. I felt like I couldn't say no to prayer, so I went to my knees with the rest of the family. Leah's dad started off by thanking God, and even reciting scriptures of the Bible from memory. The prayer session at home seemed odd to me at first, and only became even more weird when her dad started speaking in a language I couldn't understand. The language was called tongues, and I couldn't understand any of it, but the rest of her family were saying their Amens and Thank yous to God as if they understood every word. I looked around at all the heads bowed and eyes closed, except for her two younger brothers, and went from feeling out of place to being intrigued at how they seemed to be having church without being in one. I had said my prayers plenty of times before, but never like this.

Once prayer was over, they got up off their knees, and went back to what they were doing as if nothing had *happened. Leah's dad got off his knees and walked over to me and introduced himself as Minister Wilder. He asked if it was okay if he put his hands on my head to say a few words over me. I didn't know if he sensed the pain I was going through living with Mrs. Rice and thought I needed extra prayer, but I told him it was fine, and stood there accepting prayer. Once he had finished, he looked me in my eyes and told me I would speak to many in the future. I wasn't sure if he meant the word of God, or something else but I wanted to laugh out loud at the thought. Was he a prophet or something able to see into my future?*

Leah's mom stood up from her chosen place on the floor. She was a petite woman with a "larger than life" smile. I was intrigued by her eyes. They were green, and I had never seen green eyes on a black person before. She was sweet when she spoke and introduced herself as Mrs. Wilder, and I could tell Leah and her siblings were lucky to have her as a mom. I knew I needed to go so I said my goodbyes to the family and headed out the door.

"Your dad is tripping," I said to Leah as I headed down the stairs of the front porch, towards the gate.

"If you say so," she said laughing. "Just meet me back here in the morning and we can walk to school together." I told Leah that I would see her the next day not wanting to sound excited as I ran quickly down the street. I felt good about my new friendship.

Moving from house to house, I never had the opportunity to make lasting friendships, so I grew excited thinking about a possible friendship with Leah. Starsky was standing outside in front as I approached the house.

"You are in trouble, Mrs. Rice has been looking for you." I knew what was coming and thoughts began to rush my *mind. I could run away now and never look back, but I couldn't just leave Starsky. I could run back to Leah's house I thought, but say what? "I'm getting beat, please help me"?*

"Where have you been?" Mrs. Rice's voice could be heard coming through the screened front door. She had seen me, it was too late to start running. I would just have to go in and face the consequences that came with not coming immediately to the house after school.

When I got in the house Mrs. Rice told me we were heading out for dinner. I knew exactly what that meant and was thankful it happened today. The foster care check had come, which meant I may have been saved. One positive every month was that when the check came, Mrs. Rice always took us to one of the local restaurants in town, usually the buffet, for dinner. Every now and then she would let us pick where we wanted to eat. It was my favorite time of the month in her home.

During dinner Mrs. Rice appeared off. She wasn't complaining like usual, but she wasn't talking much either. Her eyes looked glazed over, and she didn't eat much of her food. I should have known something wasn't right when she didn't yell at me for not coming straight to the house after school.

Not much was said by any of us during dinner or dessert. Once finished, we walked to the car and got in. Starsky got in the front seat, while I buckled up in the back. Mrs. Rice stayed quiet most of the drive back to the house, and so did we. Two blocks from the house, Mrs. Rice let out a pained scream.

"I can't see," she yelled, as her car started to bounce off the parked cars on the busy street. Her car finally slowed *down until it was almost at a halt. Mrs. Rice wasn't saying*

anything nor moving, and people were rushing to her

Buick, opening doors, trying to get to the brakes and

completely stop the car from moving. What had just

happened? Was Mrs. Rice okay? Was she dead? Why

wasn't she moving? I was numb, I didn't feel sadness,

nor sorrow; I felt nothing.

The ambulance arrived and rushed us to the hospital.

Within a few hours, Joyce was there to pick us up. She

once again told us everything would be okay. I didn't care

what she had to say but knew I didn't just want to be

"okay" anymore. I had become a witness to what "okay"

looked like, and we definitely weren't okay. Starsky and I

sat quietly as we traveled to a respite foster home to stay

until they could figure out what was going on with Mrs.

Rice. We didn't hear any updates for multiple days. On

the fourth day, a lady showed up at the respite home

introducing herself as our new caseworker, and just like

that Joyce was gone. No notice to us, no phone call, nothing, just gone. I didn't know if I was allowed to feel sad or if I was just supposed to accept her being gone like I had to do with so many other people that came and went from my life. I did feel something though, hell, a lot of something. I felt not only sadness, but also anger. Joyce had seen what happened to me at only five years old. Why would she want to put me through that again? Joyce leaving was a whole new set of issues I had to face that I was sure no one was going to speak to me about. I was depressed and it hit me like a ton of bricks, and once again, I had no one to talk to about my issues but the bathroom mirror.

The new caseworker didn't answer any of the questions that I asked about Joyce. I wasn't sure if she didn't know the answers, or if she was just choosing not to answer. She proceeded to tell us that Mrs. Rice was doing better and would be out of the hospital the following day.

"You can go home tomorrow," she said smiling, as if she knew that's the news Starsky and I had been waiting to hear. Like most things in life, good things like meeting Leah and her family were overshadowed by news like Mrs. Rice still being alive. I soon realized we would not be escaping that easily. From then on, I knew if anything good happened to me, bad was sure to be lurking close behind.

If God had chosen to spare her life, couldn't he just take mine instead? I was over the depression and sadness, but mainly the cruel treatment from Mrs. Rice.

I'm Done

By the time I was 14, Starsky and I had been in Mrs. Rice's home for close to five years. In that time, we continued to go to church every Sunday and Bible study most Wednesdays. At church, I can recall people praying to God for forgiveness, healing, etc., while I was praying that God would take my life, or at the least save me from the hell I was living in, but my prayers were going unanswered.

On Mrs. Rice's first hospital encounter she would return home forced to do something with a needle and blood several times a day. She would then return to the hospital only to come home with one breast removed, and soon after, the other. She never told us what was happening with her but would frequently leave her implants laying around on her dresser. I accidentally walked in on her getting dressed once and was shocked at what I saw. I had never been exposed to someone with diabetes or breast cancer, let alone seen the scars it left behind. You would think that between the two, her heart would have softened, but it appeared the sickness only made it even more hardened and cold. I'm not sure if Mrs. Rice was taking her pain out on us, but she began to make us go pick the branches from the trees that she used upside our bodies. If the branch wasn't suitable enough for the butt whooping, she made us try again until we got it right. I had prayed to God so much by this time. I didn't know what else to do anymore. I just wanted it to end, but for whatever reason, God wasn't answering my prayers.

"See if you can come to revival with us tonight," Leah asked me. I had been hanging out with her and her family a lot over the years. Their home had become my only peace. They even knew Starsky and allowed him to come around. They treated him no differently than they

did me, and that made me feel good. I would go and eat good meals there and play games with the whole family.

If they were going on outings, I was treated like the rest of the family, and they would load me up in their large van right along with everyone else. Leah's family kept me going most days without even knowing it. On the nights when I lay on the bathroom floor wanting to end it all, thoughts of Leah and her family would replay in my mind. If no one else would miss me, they surely would. Since Mrs. Rice knew that Leah's dad was a minister, she allowed me to hang out with them often and even go to revival. Mrs. Rice knew their family went to church even more than she did. It was most likely out of obligation that she allowed me to go. I would use that to my advantage and continuously remind her that Leah's dad was a minister in hopes she would say yes when I asked to go places with them.

I probably should have been excited about revival, but that's not what had me excited. I was happy she said I could go so I didn't have to sit in the apartment doing nothing, or waiting around for Mrs. Rice to get mad at me about nothing. Even if it only meant being away for a few hours, I would take it.

"He said to them, 'Because of your little faith, for truly I say to you, if you have faith like a grain the size of a mustard seed, you will say move mountain, 'move from here to there,' and it will move, and nothing will be impossible for you,'" The pastor spoke loudly. He spoke with so much passion. He jumped up and down, shouting and praising God. The whole Church was standing, clapping, and shouting because of the gospel he was preaching.

"I want every child in this church tonight to come to the front if ye have even a grain of faith." I wasn't sure what

came over me, but I jumped up without hesitation. I felt like God himself said stand and go. Normally, I would have been too shy to be front and center, but I did have faith, so I went up. Young children and teens crowded all around the pulpit. Once it became too crowded, I slid further back in the large crowd of children.

I wanted to do what the pastor said, I just didn't need to be front and center while doing it. As the pastor began to speak and pray over us, I lowered my head and closed my eyes in an attempt to really focus on what he was saying. My thoughts eventually started to drift away from my problems, and to the words he was delivering. Faith the size of a mustard seed was replaying over and over as the pastor preached on.

"If you believe and have even a little faith, know that God can and will deliver you from anything you may be going through." Was he talking to me? Did this man I didn't

know standing in the pulpit in front of us know my struggles?

"On the count of three, I am going to run my hands over this crowd of young people." All the pews were empty, and most of the congregation was standing by now. The Church roared even louder in praise, as the pastor began counting. "One!" the pastor yelled. "Two…" he shouted even louder. "Three." That was the last thing I remember right before everything went dark.

I awoke to ushers fanning my body and moving my skirt back down over my knees, before lifting me up off the ground I had collapsed on. As I was assisted with standing to my feet, I looked around to see children all around me being lifted up off the ground just as I had been. I had seen things like this happen on TV, but never in real life. I always thought that people were faking for the cameras or the church when they would fall on the floor or "catch the Holy Ghost" as it was called. After this event, I never again questioned there being a God, because I had experienced Him for myself. Even if He did not always answer me, He was real. I just had to keep calling on Him and figure out how to reach Him again like tonight, so that I could leave Mrs. Rice's house for good. I went back to the apartment feeling like a new person. No longer would fear be an emotion that I felt when I was around her. I could never hate her, but other emotions had definitely engulfed my heart for her, and something had to change.

Over the next few weeks things didn't change. Mrs. Rice continued to talk bad to me, even telling me I would grow up to be nothing more than barefoot and pregnant. I found this funny, but also sad all at the same time. I didn't pay boys much attention, and they didn't pay attention to me either. The only reason I even talked to them was because I knew if I didn't, I would surely be teased even *more. Mike was never really into me and had moved on to the next girl, and the other boys didn't want to talk to me, just glance at what I was carrying right below my back. The thought of sex literally made me sick to my stomach. To possibly have sex, get pregnant and put a child through what I was going through? Never! I never wanted to have kids and that was that.*

"Starsky today is the day. I am going to tell Mrs. Rice I want to leave."

"You've been saying that forever, sis," Starsky looked at me in disbelief, but I believe a part of him knew there was some truth in what I was saying that day.

"I know, but I'm done, and I mean it this time."

"If you go tell her you want to move, sis, I'm going to tell her I want to move too."

I stood there for what felt like forever looking from the kitchen to the living room. I couldn't see her, but I knew she was in there with her feet propped up as usual stretched out in her recliner watching TV. I had stood in that same spot a lot over the years, dreaming of exactly what I was going to do, but this time I was determined. I had never been able to muster up enough courage to follow through, but this time was different. I had grown tired of the countless talent shows in the kitchen, still gaining little to no attention from her. I was over the undeserved beatings she delivered us on a regular basis, and I was just tired of being sad all the time. The mirror had been there for me when I needed it most, but I was tired of running to it, praying it would give me something that it never did. I needed something that she clearly was unable to give me, or just choosing not to.

"Here goes nothing," I told Starsky. I closed my eyes, and counted to ten (well, maybe thirty), and had faith the size of a mustard seed before walking into the living room.

I'm sure you are wondering if I actually got enough courage that night to tell her I wanted to move, and the answer is, yes. Surprisingly enough she never even moved from her recliner. She sat there and had the nerve to ask me two questions that I will never forget.

"Do you think someone else will love you and your brother like I have, and do you think someone else will give you everything you have here?" I wasn't sure if she was serious, or if those were trick questions, because there could be no way she really thought she had given me or Starsky a good life over the years.

After she said what she needed to say with nothing in return from me, she grew quiet. Since I had nothing more to say I turned and slowly walked back to my room, praying she wasn't following in behind me. Later I wondered if she had been just as tired of me as I was of her by this point because she didn't put up a fight. Whatever crossed her mind that night or afterward, she never spoke it out loud. Even if she had, I would not have cared as long as she called the caseworker to take us away.

I often hear the saying, "nothing comes without a price," and in this case that was definitely true. The journey with Mrs. Rice was finally coming to an end, but as we all know, in life, when one journey ends, another begins. I just prayed that whatever was to come for me was nothing like the past five years.

Nana

The saddest part of leaving Mrs. Rice's home was walking away from Starsky. He never joined me in my rally to leave, so when I left, I left alone. I assume fear got the best of him—too afraid to tell Mrs. Rice he wanted to leave. With him being close to age 18, I knew it was only a matter of time before he was off on his own. All I could do was pray he would be okay and one day we would reunite once again. For now, this next chapter in my life would be part of my journey that I would have to walk alone.

After leaving Mrs. Rice, I was broken. I wasn't broken because I had to leave her, because that actually made me happy. I was broken because I was leaving the only family that seemed to care about me and that was Leah and her family. I knew that I was doing what was best for me, but it still hurt. I didn't have the heart to give them real goodbyes and decided to just leave to face whatever was next for me.

My next move was to a group home for what was said would be an unknown amount of time. My caseworker had warned me if I left Mrs. Rice's house this was my only option because there were no homes willing or able at the time to take in a preteen-aged child. I still knew that this was my only opportunity to get away, so I packed more trash bags, prepared to go wherever. I had come to her with practically nothing but left with way more baggage than any child should have to.

The group home wasn't the best, but it also wasn't the worst. I ended up living there for less than 6 months. Group home living was nothing like living in a foster home. Your days were planned out, you were told what to eat, how much you could eat, and even had set times when you were allowed to eat. Outside was a privilege *that had to be earned and that was still up to the staff and on their time if they actually chose to take you out or not. I cried silent tears in the group home, not for taking beatings, but for a different reason—I felt as if I was on lockdown with no one to save me. I felt as if I was given a jail sentence with no release date. This was a time in my life that, although shorter-lived than some of my other experiences, I wouldn't want for any child to have to go through. Unfortunately, foster children are forced to live in group homes all the time at alarming rates when there are no foster homes or biological families to take them in. In my case, it was still better than living with Mrs. Rice. Even though the situation was not ideal, I still considered myself lucky. The staff treated us well for the most part, and didn't abuse us in any way, so that in itself was a win for me. There of course was drama, like there was everywhere, but I learned to lay low and avoid it at all costs. This seemed to make my time go a little quicker than I'm sure it did some of the other children. For the children who started trouble, their time there seemed to double because no home wanted a child that started trouble of any sort. Families didn't care why a child was troubled, they just knew they didn't want it in their home.*

When the time arrived to depart the group home, I moved to yet another foster home. I would live in this home for a short time as well, but would experience many emotions, and learn many lessons in my short stay.

My new foster mom's name was NaNa, or at least that's what everyone called her. She was around Mrs. Rice's age, but they were complete opposites. NaNa was short, not even standing 4 foot 11 inches tall. She was thick in a lot of areas, and in a short time I would learn why. NaNa loved to cook and feed people. Whether she knew you or not, if you were hungry and even if you were not hungry, she was feeding you. NaNa would walk around the kitchen, cooking and smiling while singing and humming her favorite gospel tunes as she prepared her meals. Her house always smelled of something good to eat.

Nana had five foster children in her large home at the time I lived there, including myself. To my surprise, she never screamed at any of us nor lifted a hand to strike us. It wasn't like we were the best group of girls. I'm sure we were more trouble than some of the other girls she had taken in over her many years of fostering.

Everyone in the area knew NaNa and loved her. People stopped by all the time to check in on her and her husband. NaNa was married but us kids rarely talked to her husband because all he did was sleep. He slept so much that people around the city called him "Sleepy." To this day, I don't know if Sleepy had an actual condition that caused him to sleep all the time, or if he was just that tired all the time. It wouldn't have surprised me if this was *the case because I'm sure a house full of girls would*

make anyone tired.

By the time I reached Nana and Sleepy's home, my heart

had become hardened and cold. I couldn't trust the words

of anyone. I had lived in more houses than some people

live in in a lifetime and had gotten used to not saying

proper goodbyes. NaNa seemed like she was trustworthy

enough, but I told myself that I wouldn't open up to her or

anyone ever again. I tried it once at five, and it got me

nowhere. People used vulnerability against you. I had

seen people fail when they became vulnerable, and I had

decided this would never be me again.

Living with NaNa was cool because she lived in the big

bright yellow house on the corner. Most people either

knew her, or at least knew the big yellow house. Days

and nights in her home were filled with all sorts of

adventures. The newness of it all was better than any group home.

Nana's home also came with the type of drama that I hadn't had to experience much of up to this point. I was now living in an actual house again, and not a group home with girls my age, which meant trouble.

At the group home, I avoided girls involved in drama at all costs, but in Nana's house this was impossible. Girls living so closely together and having to share rooms and interact even if they didn't want to meant unavoidable issues. Arguments over clothes, hair products, the way you looked at someone, all became regular everyday issues for me. Every issue big or small made me worry I would eventually have to fight over it.

Candy was one of us five girls that lived in the house. She had been with Nana for several years by the time I arrived there. She was my age, but always acted way older, and seemed to believe she was in charge of everything and everyone. The younger girls in the house listened to her because she was older and maybe because they may have thought they had no other option.

Candy had your typical foster child story, like so many of us in care during the 80s and 90s. Her mom was on drugs, and before she knew what was happening, the system had come in and swept her and her siblings out of the home.

They probably never even knew it was coming, just like Starsky and I. I remember Candy the most because of her attitude. It was so bad. Most of the time people chose not to deal with her, including myself. I could tell being in foster care had destroyed her. She was cold to most people, and most of the time downright mean. Foster care seemed to have hardened her heart, just as it had done mine over the years. I guess in that aspect, Candy and I were a lot alike.

Candy's appearance reminded me a lot of my own. Her complexion was about two shades darker than mine, and her self-esteem appeared low at times because of this. Maybe she felt the same way about her deep dark skin as I felt about mine.

In front of people, she acted as if she had all the confidence in the world, and no one could tell her anything, but I knew what low self-esteem looked like, and I knew what it felt like, because I too suffered from it. I knew deep inside she didn't really feel confident. I would often hear her complaining about how ugly she was. I never asked her, but oftentimes wondered if Candy cried when she looked in the mirror just as I had done so many times before, hoping and wishing some of the blackness could just be washed away.

"Come on," Candy stated to me as she ran down the stairs, and past Sleepy. It was 9:30pm on a Saturday and we were on our way to the grocery store for our weekly late-night snack run. This was my favorite weekly activity. The younger girls in the house followed close behind Candy as we ran to NaNa's large van. Once NaNa was in the driver's seat, she did her routine of passing each of us our few dollars to be spent on whatever we wanted. This small gesture on NaNa's part was something that I always remembered even after I moved. Candy was smiling and in such a great mood that she didn't even try and swipe one of my dollars like she often did. I always allowed her to take a little of my money or offer her my snacks because I knew that would prevent any issues with her. The younger girls would offer Candy some of their money, but she would always refuse. She would be *hard on the younger girls, but she always looked out for them to make sure no one was taking advantage of them. I assume maybe that's why they looked up to her.*

When we arrived at the grocery store, we ran around collecting all the Hot Cheetos, honey buns, sour candy, soda, and whatever else our few dollars could buy. NaNa always gave us about 15 minutes to get our junk and get back to the front of the store, but it never took us longer than about 10 minutes to spend our 2 to 3 dollars.

"Come on, girl," Candy said, sliding something in her pocket. Candy had asked me to go around the store with her, so of course I did, even though I wanted this time to myself. Candy was stealing and I wasn't sure why because she had money to buy what she was taking. I didn't ask her any questions because I preferred the nice Candy. I thought to myself, "Please don't let the police stop us," as we checked out and headed to the front of

the store. "The Awakening" was coming on television and I dang-sure wasn't planning on missing it because of Candy. It was a continuation from the previous week, and we all planned to take over NaNa's bedroom floor and watch it like we did every Saturday night with our snacks.

Thank goodness there were no police waiting to stop us, and soon we were back in the van heading to NaNa's house. As we all prepared for the show to come on. Candy threw me some of the extra treats she had in her pocket. She was sharing her snacks, as opposed to taking mine. I considered this a good day, and I was always thankful for the good days.

Things had been going okay in NaNa's house for the most part. I had become a little mouthy because that's what I saw the other girls do, and I had even started to dress showing more of the body I continued to develop. I figured if I couldn't beat Candy, I may as well join her.

NaNa had tried talking to me about being my own person, but she didn't know what it was like to be a teen. She was old.

NaNa had lots of great grandkids, or at least that's what she called them, and one in particular had caught my eye in the few months I had been living there. CJ was his name, and he had to be at least 6 to 7 years older than me, but I didn't care. He was tall, dark, and handsome. He didn't pay any attention to me, but I definitely paid him some. Boys had recently started to gain my attention since I had been living in NaNa's house.

I heard NaNa say he was coming over, so I put on my cute, fitted body dress in preparation to see him, and then headed to the basement with the other girls.
I heard CJ upstairs talking to NaNa and knew it was only a matter of time before he and his boys would be headed down. The girls and I were watching music videos and

dancing. I started shaking my butt to the music even faster, like Candy was doing, when I saw the guys watching from the bottom of the stairs. CJ and his boys watched for a quick moment then told Candy she was too young to be dancing like she was. Candy was like a little sister to CJ, but he wasn't like a big brother to me. I kept shaking my butt while his friends stared on.

"Come on y'all," CJ told his boys as he led the way back up the stairs.

Once I walked upstairs, I noticed they had departed and were not coming back. Frustrated, I headed back downstairs. Candy decided to go hangout outside, but I was tired and didn't feel like being bothered anymore. I laid on the couch frustrated, thinking how I hadn't been able to get attention, even in a fitted dress.

Nana's youngest girls continued to dance around the basement as I relaxed, looking at the girls in the music video getting the complete opposite reaction of what I had just gotten. This sucks, I thought, as I drifted off to sleep.

"NOOOOOOOOOOOO," I heard Candy screaming and crying upstairs some time later. The screams were so intense I awoke frightened. I immediately ran upstairs to see what was going on. Candy was yelling words I couldn't understand while NaNa attempted to hold her close as she herself was crying and screaming, "My God."

I hadn't the slightest idea as to what could possibly be going on. People then started rushing in and out of NaNa's home screaming something about CJ being shot and killed. I stood in shock, unable to move. Just today, he was in NaNa's house, and in her basement. What did they mean dead? He couldn't be dead. I had just seen him smiling and very much alive. This had to be one bad dream.

It was confirmed quickly that it wasn't a dream at all, CJ had indeed been shot and killed not far from NaNa's house. People crowded the streets in front of the house, trying to figure out what had happened, but the reality was he was gone. I hadn't known him as long as Candy and the other foster kids had, so my sadness was for them and NaNa because I saw the hurt and pain that couldn't be hidden.

CJ would be my first encounter with death, but certainly not my last. His death would be the beginning of the realization that we live, and we die. CJ's death, just like Greenwood Cemetery, would stay on my mind daily. When CJ died, I realized death was not just for the sick and old. He was young, healthy, and full of life, but just as it had come for him it would do the same for me. My fear of death grew stronger after this.

CJ's death made Candy even more angry and mean, which I didn't think was even possible. She couldn't hide her pain or stop crying over the next week. She lashed out at me and even the younger girls for no reason. She definitely seemed to take his death the hardest.

CJ was buried about a week later, but I didn't go to the funeral. I chose not to go or ask any questions. I did wonder if he had been buried in Greenwood Cemetery by Wanda's house, but I never asked. NaNa's house was busy with visitors checking in on her for a while after that. I saw strength and faith when I looked into her face. She looked so broken and still walked around thanking God for his goodness and mercy. She was praising God even through her storm. I had seen people praising God all the time, but never while actually in the storm. After the funeral, life eventually went back to normal, but a piece of NaNa and Candy was gone   .

As NaNa prepared dinner and cleaned the kitchen her house phone began to ring. She let it ring several times, probably debating if she was in the mood to talk. Once she decided to answer, I couldn't hear what she was saying, but a smile spread across her face. It was the first smile I had seen since CJ had been killed. She looked from the kitchen to the dining room where I was sitting at the table and told me the phone call was for me. I had to look around twice to make sure she was talking to me. I hadn't received any calls at NaNa's house the whole time I had been living there. Heck, I never received phone calls in any house I lived in. As NaNa handed me the phone, thoughts began to rush through my head of who could possibly be calling me. What could this be about? Had something happened to Starsky? NaNa was smiling so couldn't be that. I slowly walked to the kitchen taking the receiver out of her hand.

"Hello?" I spoke into the phone, just above a slight whisper.

"Hello, Via," the soft voice on the other end said. Who was this on the other end calling me by my nickname, I wondered. "This is your Aunt Linda."

Linda was Wanda and my mom's sister. I knew who she was but not very well. She went on to tell me she was taking classes to become a foster parent and I would be able to come and live with her and her boys soon. I wanted to get excited but knew better than to just believe words.

"I can't promise you it will happen overnight, but I promise you it will happen. I love you," she said.

I couldn't say it back, but I felt in my heart she meant it. I wondered where she had been all this time, and why hadn't she gotten me before now? Why now? I had been in the system for almost 10 years and was over it at this point, so in a lot of ways it didn't matter why now. I could only hope that now my depression would come to an end. No longer being in the care of complete strangers would be the start of something good. NaNa smiled and told me everything was going to be okay when she saw me lost in thought. Was she right though? Would I actually be okay?

That night I prayed that God held my aunt to her word, and if I remained in foster care, I prayed it would be kinship care with her.

New Home

My aunt stayed true to her word. Not long after our talk, I was headed to live with her and my cousins. After 10 years in the system, I would still not be with my biological mom, but another one of her sisters was once again willing to step in and take on what should not have been their responsibility.

 NaNa gave me the biggest hug, even though I stood there not reciprocating it.

"You are going to be just fine, baby," she said.

For some reason, this was the first time I believed those words. I couldn't bring myself to tell NaNa goodbye or that I would miss her, let alone that she would never be forgotten but it was definitely how I felt. I think in some strange way she knew by the smile she gave me as I left *out her front door for the last time. She had been the first foster parent I had encountered that gave me hope that not everyone was out to collect the little check that came with taking me in. She had shown me that a true believer praises God even when caught up in the storms of life. God had placed me in her home for many reasons, even if the time there would only last a season. It would be a season that I would cherish for a lifetime and forever be grateful for, even if in that moment I didn't understand it all yet.*

Aunt Linda pulled up to Nana's house to pick me up in the flyest car I had ever seen. It was a two-door, bright red, low-to-the-ground 1990 Firebird. I tried acting as if the Firebird wasn't the coolest car I had ever seen, but I'm sure the smile that spread from ear to ear as the wind hit my face was an instant giveaway.

We traveled for a short time, making a few turns before turning into yet another cul-de-sac. Pulling up to the new neighborhood was like a breath of fresh air. For the first time in my life, I felt at peace with my next, and hopefully last move. It was nothing like the cul-de-sac Aunt Wanda lived in. It was smaller and not creepy at all. There were no churches, no cemeteries, and only about eight houses surrounding hers.

I knew which house was Auntie's by the teenage boys playing basketball in the driveway. I recognized one of the boys as Aunt Linda's son, Taka. I remembered seeing family pictures of Aunt Linda and her boys in Wanda's house when I lived there, but only had super vague memories of them in person.

Auntie parked the Firebird on the street to keep from interrupting the boys' game. One of the boys playing basketball caught my eye. He had to be about 6'4" with a slender frame. I could tell puberty was hitting him hard by the pimples that covered his face. Boys had continued to become more intriguing to me and my plan was to get to know him.

"Hey cousin," Taka said as I got out of the car.

The way he greeted me was if I had just returned from the store or somewhere, and not the first time he was actually seeing me. I could tell he was a pretty boy. His teeth were the whitest I had ever seen. Those along with his fresh new tennis shoes, and haircut were a giveaway his appearance was very important to him. He was as dark as mine, if not darker, but he had a confidence I would never have carrying around this complexion of mine.

"What's up cousin?" I replied, smiling back.

I followed Aunt Linda into the house making sure not to look in the direction of the friend. I could sense that his eyes were on me, but I had no plans of looking back. As we walked through the front door, and up the short flight of stairs, Sheem, Auntie's youngest son, moved quickly in our direction.

"Hey Via!" Sheem greeted me while running out the front door and to the game happening in the driveway.

I wasn't sure how he knew my childhood nickname, but him saying it immediately made me feel even more like I belonged. They didn't pretend to fuss over being happy about my presence but smiled genuine smiles of approval.

Aunt Linda showed me around the house and then to my new bedroom. Once I walked in my room I wanted to scream with happiness, but I knew I could never show that vulnerable side of myself. Aunt Linda had purchased me a new canopy bed with golden rails, pretty pink and white bedding, and the matching gold mirror and chair vanity set. It was as if she already knew what I liked and wanted me to feel welcomed. It worked because the room was the last thing I needed to see. I officially felt at home. I felt it was what I deserved, and what was owed to me for my troubles over the years. To just finally feel at home was an indescribable feeling. It was not Auntie who owed it to me, but I felt life in general did.

Auntie lived in a split-level home that was very well decorated. Her years of working at the post office had provided a nice roof over their heads and now mine. After making sure I felt comfortable, Aunt Linda told me she wasn't feeling well and was going to lay down.

"Can I go outside with my cousins?" Aunt Linda looked at me with a look that made me know I had asked a silly question.

She let me know that this was now my home, and I could always go outside. Home wasn't a word I had myself used often over the years, but I was looking forward to it becoming a frequent word in my vocabulary. I could get used to this new life, and for sure my new home.

"Your cousin is cute," I heard Taka's friend say, as I stood inside the front door watching them shoot the ball.

Taka gave him a side eye before letting him know that I was family and very much off-limits. I acted as if I heard nothing and ran outside to jump in their game of 21.

After shooting some air balls, I stepped aside to watch them play.

"I'm Josh," he said, introducing himself as he stood in front of me shooting his foul shot.

"I'm out," Sheem yelled as he ran around the corner heading somewhere deeper into the neighborhood.

"I'll be back," Taka said, walking inside the house, but not before giving Josh another look.

Taka was barely inside the door before Josh immediately struck up a conversation.

"Have you met Crystal and the rest of the crew?" I did not have the slightest idea who Josh was talking about, so I just told him no. He saw me arrive just today, so he had to know I'd had no time to meet anyone. He just laughed and said, "You will, they live in the neighborhood."

Josh asked me a few more questions that I chose to ignore because I wasn't sure how much he knew about my life in foster care. Either way, I did not want to lie about my past or talk about it. He must have noticed my silence because he stopped questioning me.

"What y'all talking about?" Auntie said, giggling from a window right above where we stood.

Her bedroom window was located right above the driveway, and she had probably heard our whole conversation.

"Nothing, Auntie," I yelled back at the window, laughing.

I made sure to take mental note to never say anything I did not want Auntie to hear while in the driveway. Josh and I talked a little more before he had to get home. Josh said goodbye and him, and his bowed legs took off in the same direction that Sheem had gone.

Josh was right and the summer entering into my freshman year was the best summer of my life. I met Tiarra, Crystal, Kee Kee, and Amber. I understood then why Josh had laughed when he had asked if I had met the girls. They were a mess, but in good ways. They all had their own unique style and personalities. They were funny, smart, and so much more.

Tiarra was extremely goofy, but also extremely smart. She always had us laughing, while Kee Kee wore nothing but the best designer clothes and shoes. Crystal had that light skinned complexion that boys craved, and Amber turned out to be one of the best cheerleaders I would ever meet. Most of the time I felt as if I wasn't cool enough or pretty enough to hang out with them, but they allowed me to, so I did. I assumed they knew my family *situation, but they never spoke on it, which was*

something I was thankful for. Low self-esteem still had

me questioning a lot of things about myself, but I tried not

to let that weakness show in front of them or anyone.

I went to parties with the girls when Auntie would allow it,

and we all frequently walked to nearby stores, and fast-

food restaurants in the area. We just enjoyed being

teenagers. We had plans to live it up the last summer

before high school, and that's exactly what we did.

Freshman year was a good year. I did not know at the

time, but I was entering a predominantly white school

with less than 15 black students in the entire high school.

This was something different for me as I had mainly been

in diverse schools all my previous years.

For the most part, everyone liked me and I was exposed

to very few instances of racism. The other girls had

attended elementary and middle school with the same group of kids, so they were already well-known. Once people found out I was Taka's cousin they immediately seemed accepting. Even if they weren't accepting at first, they didn't show it or speak on it.

In the new school I wasn't teased for my dark skin color, my big nose and forehead, or any of my many other flaws. This may have had something to do with Taka himself being the color of dark chocolate, around 6 foot 4 inches, and weighing close to 200 lbs. He was definitely someone that when you saw him you automatically knew not to mess with him or his family. I can only assume that's why his nickname was Tank.

Although being teased wasn't a concern, excelling in my classes was another story. All I could seem to do was manage to stay afloat. This kept me away from the happening parties and overnights with the girls.

Academics were something that Auntie took very seriously. Either you came home with decent grades, or you stayed in the house. Let's just say I stayed in quite a bit my freshman year leading into sophomore year. My mind was never able to focus long enough to be good in any subject other than P.E. and art. Honestly, I really wasn't even good in art class, but the teacher was nice which made the class fun and at least passable for me.

Education of any sort was not for me until my sophomore year. That year, I started an English class with Mr. S. He was not only the high school English teacher, but also the head boys basketball coach. He was reserved and soft-spoken at all times, unless he was on the court assisting his team to a win. Something about Mr. S's demeanor and the way he spoke was like no other teacher I had ever encountered. He was always willing to lend an extra hand, and never looked down on students when they didn't understand.

It was in high school and in his class that I knew I wanted to become a teacher. I wanted to talk and have people listen the way they did to him. I had it all planned out in my head and just needed to make it happen. I would attend an all-black university studying education. I would join that sorority and so much more, but first I needed to be accepted into a college. This meant I needed to concentrate long enough to graduate high school with more than just passable grades.

Josh and I started dating and became inseparable. I was dating the star point guard at my school, and things were definitely as they should be. I had even noticed that the sadness I had been experiencing prior to moving to the area was somewhat fading away. I had moments of unexplained sadness but for the most part things seemed to be looking up. With a plan for the future, family, and a

man, life was feeling pretty good.

"Hey cousin, who's that white girl in your room?" Taka

laughed at my question as he made his sandwich.

We stood in the kitchen laughing as I waited for Josh to

sneak out and stop by. His parents were very strict, so

him sneaking was our only option outside of school

hours.

"Mind yo business, Flo diva," Taka said laughing. Either

the nickname he had just given me or my comment about

the white girl had him laughing and showing off all his

pearly whites. Once he was in the bathroom and out of

sight, I took that as my time to go in his room and get the

answers I wanted.

The girl in his room looked up at me as I entered but continued lying where she was on his bed. She looked a little too comfortable, so I figured I'd join her. I would get the answers one way or another to the questions Taka chose to ignore. Taka and Sheem had become more like brothers than cousins to me. I needed to see if she was worthy to occupy his time, let alone the bed she was laying on.

"Hey girl, I'm Dovia, what's your name?" She smiled at me and told me that her name was Kindle.

"So, you and Taka dating or something?" Kindle laughed looking unsure as to whether she even knew the answer to that question herself.

Her smile instantly gave me good vibes, so I decided not to push it too much with the questions, at least for now. I switched up the convo and decided to talk about school.

We apparently went to the same high school and were even in the same grade. I had assumed that she was a year older like Taka since I didn't remember seeing her around school, but she wasn't. We talked about classes, and how she had been friends with Crystal since elementary. I decided then she was okay with me. She seemed like a cool enough person that I did not mind getting to know her. For now, I approved of her.

"Flo diva, Josh here, now gone somewhere," Taka said walking into his room eating his sandwich.

"I will see you around, girlie," I said with a smile.

I eased out of the bedroom to go and greet Josh at the door. Josh and I decided to go across the hall to Sheem's empty room. He was gone and I knew Auntie was at work. I figured if Auntie came home, Josh would be thrown out of the room with the quickness. Taka and Josh were best friends, but Auntie was no fool, and I planned on taking no chances. One thing her and Aunt Wanda had in common was they were definitely not to be messed with.

Josh and I sat on the floor playing mortal combat. We continued to battle back and forth, but I knew he was letting me win as we sat shoulder to shoulder, controllers in hand.

We had been close to one another before, but never this close. Josh was so close I could feel him staring at me even though I was trying not to acknowledge it. Once our eyes actually met, Josh leaned in for a kiss that I chose not to stop. I had never kissed a boy before, let alone been this close to one since Brandon when I was five.

I closed my eyes and felt my heart racing faster and faster. Josh continued to lean in closer until our lips met. Once they met, the fireworks that I expected to go off with a first kiss just didn't happen. It was nothing like I had seen in movies or even imagined.

He decided to take my bottom lip into his mouth, only his nibble became a bite, and that bite made me scream out in pain. Blood had begun dripping from my lip as I ran to the bathroom sink. I ran water over my lip to try and stop the bleeding.

"You good, Flo diva?" Taka was asking from his room.

"Yea, I'm good," I said, hurrying to reply.

I wasn't really good, but I didn't need him coming to check on me.

Was it my lack of experience or his that now had me washing blood from my bottom lip? I was officially and completely embarrassed, and knew it was time for Josh to leave. I knew that kissing was something more intimate and had broken my own rule about not kissing, but never again.

Josh and I hung out a few more times after the incident, but soon realized a relationship wasn't for us.

Josh would move on and start dating the star of the girls basketball team, and for now I would remain single. I assumed a boyfriend added something to my life that I just knew had to be the reason for my happiness. I prayed God would send another man my way. My relationship with Josh may have ended, but another relationship started up strong and heavy.

Kindle and I became best friends that were inseparable. We started registering for the same classes, cheating off one another's homework, and sneaking out of school to go to lunch together. Kindle's dad became like a dad to me and her grandparents were the grandparents I never had. Wherever I was, she was there and vice versa. Even when her relationship ended with Taka, we remained best friends. I not only had my own biological family now, I had extended family once again.

God had taken my years of feeling left out with no family, and gave me double for my troubles. Life was going well for the moment, or so I thought.

"Via come here," Auntie called out to me from her bed as I walked down the hall. Auntie had started looking more worn out in recent months, and I assumed she was tired from working so much at the post office.

"Come lay with me," she said with a smile. I did as Auntie asked and curled up next to her on the bed. We laid quiet for a short while before, "I have cancer," came out of her mouth. Those words started replaying over and over in my head as she began talking to me. She was saying other words but all I heard was Cancer. I couldn't cry in front of her, so I just silently listened and held back my emotions. What was God trying to prove? Why was my Auntie sick? None of this seemed fair.

"I'm going to fight this, Via, but if I die the boys are taken care of, and I have left something for you as well." I didn't want or need anything. Aunt Linda had made sure we had food, shelter, and even the right amount of discipline. Most of all, she showed me what it was to have unconditional love from family. I just needed her to be okay.

That night I did the only thing I knew to do and that was to pray. My prayers to God became stronger in the weeks and months that followed. I needed a miracle and I needed it soon, but in the months that followed, her health got worse and her body weakened. She stopped talking as much and would look at me and try to smile as

I snuck past her bedroom door to look in on her. She was growing tired and weaker by the day, and it was showing on her face. I wasn't sure if God was hearing my prayers at all, and I didn't know what else to do.

Not Ready for Goodbye

I sat on the school bus knowing that something wasn't right. It was something about these extra beautiful sunny days that never ended well for me. The cars lining the cul-de-sac were the first thing I noticed as I sat looking out the window of the bus.

As the bus slowed to a complete stop, I got off and began slowly walking the short distance from the corner to our house. Taka sitting on the front porch with his head hanging low was the first thing I noticed. He never looked up, just sat there as people stood close by. I could tell by the different expressions that covered their faces that something was definitely wrong. Things began to grow even more concerning as I got closer and saw Sheem. The look on his face was one that I had never seen before. At the time I didn't realize that it was the look of unexplainable, unbearable pain trapped inside not *knowing how to escape. I walked to where Taka sat, but he said nothing. He continued looking towards the ground. I looked back to Sheem and he too said nothing. I walked through the front door of our house and got the confirmation that I didn't want. Something definitely wasn't right. Wanda's face appeared, which shocked me even more. I hadn't seen much of her in the year I had been living with Aunt Linda, which was okay with me. I had never really forgiven her for throwing Starsky and I out the way she did all those years ago, but here we stood, eye to eye. When I saw the pastor of a nearby church following close behind Wanda, my heart sank. I knew him being there was not a good sign. He looked at me and gave me a sympathetic look as he walked out the front door. "What is going on?" I thought to myself, afraid to ask out loud. No one was saying anything and my head and my thoughts were spinning. "Where is Auntie and is she okay?" was all I could think.*

"Via, Linda is gone." The dark truth was being spoken out loud by Wanda.

"She passed away while you all were at school today." My heart felt like it literally could stop at any moment. What was Wanda saying? Her expression softened some, but once again no tears were flowing. Maybe she had cried them all out before we arrived knowing she needed to stay strong for us, but my prior strength was weakening from the news. I felt that if I continued to stand, my legs would give out on me at any moment. My heart picked up its pace even faster as I walked past Wanda not saying a word. I walked up the few stairs that led to the living room debating whether to go left or right. I wanted to go to the right, in the direction of Aunt Linda's bedroom, just to confirm she was no longer there, but I couldn't. My feet instead led me to the left where I sat down on the couch. My mind was going in so many directions that I didn't know what to think. People were

coming in and out of the house slowly, looking saddened by the news. I would hear sorry for your loss here and there, but my mind was elsewhere. As I sat looking out the window, I could see Taka's car speeding off in the direction that led out the cul-de-sac. I couldn't begin to imagine what he was going through or even thinking. I never had a mother so I couldn't relate firsthand, but I knew him, Sheem and Aunt Linda were very close. Taka would now be a junior in high school with no mom, and Sheem in middle school with no mother. They would now experience the pain of growing older without their mom's guidance. This made me hurt for them because while I didn't know their pain, I knew what came without a mom in my life and I wanted that pain for no one, especially them.

I started to become angry at God for them and then become angry for myself. Why was God doing this? Why would he allow me this short time out of foster care with

Auntie Linda only to take her away. I had seen him spare the life of a woman that beat me, but not spare my Auntie who helped everyone she could, whenever she could. My days of not questioning God were once again over. I needed answers and I needed them now.

The days leading up to her funeral were some of the hardest days I have ever had to face. I faced getting beat with extension cords better than I was able to deal with losing my aunt. She had been the only blood relative that had attempted to save me from a corrupt foster care system, and I was not ready to say goodbye. I do not think anyone was ready to say goodbye. The church started to crowd with mourners waiting to get one final view of her body. As I stood deep in thought, I looked around only to see that same face that had not left my memory in over 10 years. It was the same face that stood looking at me on the sidewalk as I screamed in the back of Joyce's car. The same face that had been embedded *in my brain at only five years old. The same face that was now standing in the same room as me. She looked at me and I at her.*

At that moment I knew exactly who she was. She wasn't just a stranger that had seen me kicking and screaming as I was carried out and placed in the backseat of that car. She wasn't just a saddened stranger that happened to be walking down the sidewalk at the wrong place and time and had wondered what was happening with that little boy and girl. Here after all these years stood the woman that had chosen over 10 years ago to stand on that sidewalk and say or do nothing, and because of that, I decided no words would be exchanged that day or any other. Instead we continued mourning for her sister and my aunt, and remained two strangers that crossed paths on an empty sidewalk in Greenview on a day that I will never forget. Starsky was there and had aged out of foster care. He was forced to start living life like everyone else. No exceptions were made because of his disability. He had to figure out life just like every other foster child that was now too old for the system to pretend to care about. He had decided to build a relationship with our mom and had even chosen to live with her, probably because he had no other choice. I never asked him questions and when he tried to volunteer information after we reconnected again after the funeral, I told him I didn't care. No generational curses would be broken anytime soon. It would never be that easy for me to just forgive and forget, especially not now. If she would have done her job as a mother, Aunt Linda and I could have had many years together before now.

"Dovia, you can do this. Aunt Linda loved you, and you need to say your last goodbye." I stood there alive yet feeling so dead on the inside, telling myself what I had to do.

I stood in line with everyone else waiting for my time. My mind was refusing to take a break, and my anxiety was kicking in. She is going to wake up any minute I thought over and over in my head. This was all just a bad nightmare I told myself. I stood over her casket, but she never moved, and it was not a dream. She looked like she was sleeping, like I had seen her do a lot more the sicker she became, only this time she would never awaken.

I wanted to cry as I looked down at her lifeless body. I wanted to reach in and give her a big kiss on the forehead and thank her and tell her that I loved her, but once again I did nothing. I stood in that church becoming more saddened and angrier. I had kept my mustard seed of faith and God still took my aunt. I stood unable to let out the screams that wanted to come out of me so badly. I looked at my Aunt for the last time ever and walked away. I kept all my feelings inside that day once again, never to discuss those feelings with anyone. The

overwhelming feeling of sadness that had been creeping

into me over the years that I thought was going away

completely took over my body that day. The last bit of a

chance that I had at life was gone. The day Aunt Linda

was buried, a large piece of me was too. The same

cemeteries that had haunted my thoughts now held my

Aunt and would never let her go. Depression took me

over full force that day and for many years that followed.

Back to Wanda's

Not too long after Auntie was buried, Wanda was placed in charge of the boys and the money that was left for them and me. Things immediately changed and so did our lives.

"Y'all get your stuff together, it's time to go," Wanda said, standing in the hallway of Aunt Linda's home looking in Taka and Sheem's direction.

She never once looked my way, but I assumed she had to be talking to me as well. As they finished packing up their things, I did the same in preparation for moving back into Wanda's house for the second time. She didn't actually tell me I was going, but she didn't tell me I wasn't either. What I did know was that I was not planning on being left behind, and I for sure was not wanting to go back to the group home. Wanda didn't seem pleased to *be taking any of us, but she did. She may have felt*

obligated, but I also was not planning on asking

questions. Her house had to be better than going to

strangers. I had gotten used to living with Taka and

Sheem and felt secure with them, so I could only hope

she planned to keep me as well.

Aunt Wanda had moved from her old home that had

occupied so many of my memories and was now living in

a three-story home not too far away from Greenwood. It

was a large, but an older home that she had put work into

to make her own. Taka and Sheem were given the whole

third level, which had two bedrooms, and a bathroom. I

was given the room on the middle floor across from her

room.

Wanda had married by this time, so not only were we

moving in with someone who felt like a stranger, but also

a man who actually was. Knowing that this was not

Wanda's first go at marriage, we weren't sure what to expect. She made it known loud and clear that we would not come in and interrupt her current life, or her marriage. We were told that he was bringing the money into the house as a retired firefighter and Veteran, and we were expected to respect him. Wanda made it very clear if anyone was forced to leave, it wouldn't be him. When she became upset, we had the pleasure of hearing how she had raised all her children and she did not ask to raise more.

Taka, Sheem, and I went from living carefree lives to moving to the other side of the city with an aunt that could care less if we were in her home or not. Taka had to drive us back and forth to school, because we now lived even further away from our current school. Most days we rode back to Wanda's house together but other days if Taka had practice, I would have to figure out how to make it back on my own. Thank goodness for friends because I spent a lot of time asking for rides.

The three of us tried to pick up the pieces of our broken lives and keep going but would soon learn that when you lose a person that held everything and everyone together; life isn't as simple as picking up where you left off. Taka and Sheem both seemed to become angrier with the new situation by the day and I understood why real soon. They didn't care for Eric Wanda's new husband and neither did I. Just as Wanda did, he too made it known that we were in his house and not the other way around. Taka let it be known that he was his own man, and he couldn't just come into his life making demands. I tried to stay neutral and mind my business as much as possible because I knew what would happen if Wanda grew tired of me. The results for me would be different than my cousins. Foster care was waiting to sweep me right back up, and I wanted no parts of it.

In the short time that we had been living in Wanda's home she went above and beyond not only providing a roof over our heads but transforming it into a lavish one. Once we were settled in, the renovations began. The third level was completely redone, and furnished with the best of flat screen TVs, and new furniture and accessories to match. Everything came in new, nothing used. No expense was spared in redecorating the rest of the house as well. Lots of money was being spent to make us feel at home or so we thought, and we were frequently reminded just how blessed we were.

With all the fabulous new items coming into the home, it didn't take long before we began to wonder who was actually being blessed from this new setup.

"Okay, girl, I will see you tomorrow," I said to Kindle, getting out of her small Prism. Kindle had dropped me off at home and I was grateful because looking for rides had

become torture. It had been a beautiful day so we rode with the windows down, jamming as loudly as we could to some of our favorite jams.

"Alright see you tomorrow," Kindle was yelling as she backed out of Wanda's steep driveway. She was headed to her part time job at the chicken hut. I was thankful she worked tonight so she could drop me off even though it was completely out of the way for her. I dug my keys out of the bottom of my bookbag before entering through the side door.

"Don't come into my house slamming doors," I could hear Eric yelling from their bedroom. I could tell he probably wasn't happy that his alone time was ending, and I was home from school. I knew Wanda was either at work or on the slot machines. If she was on the slots, she wasn't in town which meant she wasn't to be bothered. She wouldn't be home until late night or the next morning.

This had become a regular thing since we moved in. Aunt Wanda was jumping on the highway often, traveling to the nearest city with a casino. She might be gone a night or sometimes a whole weekend, but she was rarely sitting still at home. Wherever she was wouldn't help me now.

"I didn't slam the door," I responded back. I hadn't said it with an attitude, but still immediately started to regret my decision to say anything at all. I knew he was trying to get under my skin, and I had fallen right into the trap. Neither Taka nor Sheem were home so I knew it was best I move quickly to my room. I hadn't made it a few steps before Eric stormed out of the bedroom and stood looking down over me.

"Bitch, you don't run anything in this house, so watch how you talk to me." Thoughts started to fly through my head, and before I knew it, anger was the only emotion I felt.

Who did he think he was talking to me like this and why? I was never disrespectful to him or anyone. A side of me came out that even I didn't know I had.

"Who are you talking to?" I asked as if I didn't already know the answer. He looked me up and down, probably surprised I had even responded back before turning and walking away. I took several deep breaths because I knew this wasn't going to end well for me, then went to my room. I made sure to close my bedroom door even softer than I had the side door. I was fuming from the name he had called me and how he treated me in general, so I decided napping seemed like my next best option.

I opened my eyes to an already set sun and Wanda's voice. She had made it back home earlier than I had expected. I knew she would be coming in my room at any moment about my lack of respect in her home and to her husband. I definitely wasn't ready for it. I never wanted to make Aunt Wanda upset because I knew what that led to. The look on her face was an unpleasant one as she opened my door and told me to come out. I was hoping she hadn't been gambling because if she had, and had lost money, this really wasn't going to be good for me.

I stood in the kitchen waiting for Wanda to ask me what happened, but she never did. I was never asked because she didn't care.

"You got to go," was all she said.

"What?" I responded. "Go where?"

"That is not my problem, but you are leaving this house." It shouldn't have surprised me that I was getting put out yet again but under the circumstances it did. I knew she would be unhappy, but not to the point of putting me out.

I guess because I didn't come with a large payday for her like my cousins did, she didn't have to make it work with me. They could say how they felt, and she would complain but because she continued to steal their money thinking they wouldn't realize it, she always stopped at complaining. I once again came with no benefits and just like before was still disposable like the trash. Within a couple weeks I was back out the door and back into foster care. Being a teenager back in the system made me numb. I didn't know what was in store for me and immediately in my time of fear and need I did the only thing I knew to do and that was pray. Even when I became upset with God he was the only thing for me to lean on.

"The righteous cry out, and the LORD hears them, he delivers them from all their troubles. The Lord is close to the brokenhearted and saves those who are crushed in spirit." - Psalm 34: 17-18.

Part 2

The first part of my life just happened and none of it by choice. I happened to be born to a mom that was addicted to drugs, and I happened to never know who my father was because of this. I happened to have an aunt that had now put me out not once but twice, and another aunt that loved and took care of me as her own. This aunt gave me things that I never had before in life and as things seem to just happen, she was now gone. "I hadn't chosen foster care; it had chosen me." Foster care had a hold on me and it didn't seem like it planned on letting go anytime soon.

I think back, able to recount various events from my childhood and youth that have forever been engraved in my head and heart, but going into young adult life and then adult life was completely different. This next part of my life wouldn't entail trauma forced upon me by others, but poorly made decisions on my part that would have me wondering years later how I could allow my past to get me to the point that I felt like I needed others in order to find the happiness that was buried so deep inside of me.

Being considered almost an adult was a part of my journey in life that I was not ready for, and one that no one had taken the time to prepare me for. People didn't care that I was still a foster child at 17. Most of the time I didn't even tell people I was in foster care because of the shame I felt knowing my mom was across town somewhere living her life, while I became more and more lost in mine. I began to realize that people were good at acting as if they cared about others' lack of family and support, but oftentimes if it wasn't impacting their life personally, they didn't really care. I knew telling people my truth wouldn't change the past or my future and sympathy wasn't something I wanted or needed, so I

*carried on with my hurt buried deep inside. In this new
journey of life, I was going to have to be even stronger
than ever before and I knew it. I would no longer be a
victim, and from here on out I would be making the
decisions that would continue to hinder me or hopefully
start to help me. The hold of foster care that had been my
life would soon slowly be lifted from around me, and I
didn't even know it. I would soon be forced into situations
where sink or swim were the only two options I would
have. In some life situations, I swam like never before,
but other times life would leave me floating on top of the
water like a dead fish.*

*I had been so eager and ready to escape the pain of my
past, that I believed becoming an adult was the only way
I could do it. I would face challenges of life and love
everyday like everyone else, only being in foster care
never taught me how to handle any of the situations I
encountered. Because of this, I allowed what I thought*

was being grown to hurt me more than help me. These

decisions would have me in situations that not only hurt

me, but later in life would almost cost me my own.

Deeper into Womanhood

After departing Wanda's, I went to yet another foster home. I guess I should have felt lucky that there was a home even willing to take in a teen girl, especially one that had now actually developed an attitude from life experiences. I didn't look at it as luck at all though, in fact moving to another foster home only meant that I had to be even more prepared for whatever was to come. I didn't know if I was going to another home like NaNa's or somewhere like Mrs. Rice's house, but I knew I would be ready to defend myself at any cost. I would no longer be the scared and powerless little girl that allowed herself to be beaten upside the head and body by all objects. Those days were officially over, and that old me was officially gone.

"Here we go again," I thought, as yet another worker pulled up to take me away. This time the worker was a familiar face and not a complete stranger. Her name was Stacey, and we had initially met while I was living in the group home. I hadn't seen her in years. At the time we initially met she couldn't have been more than a few years graduated from college. During my stay in the group home, I had taken a liking to her because she seemed to care about what I had to say when most didn't. Stacey was one of the few people that made me believe foster care didn't have to be the end for me. Talking to her allowed me to see she wasn't just there for a check. I could see by the car she drove that she wasn't making a ton of money in her current position. Maybe she did actually care about us foster kids. Stacey frequently visited the campus and would check with me to see if I wanted to come to her office and talk. We would walk to the nearby house that was within a few feet of the group home to talk. The house acted as the office for her and two other social workers. When I wasn't in the mood to talk, Stacey would let me do little odd jobs in the house that I enjoyed to keep me busy. I did anything the office needed just so I could be out of the locked facility, and away from the chaos of the group home, even if only for a little while. Talks of my dreams of one day leaving Decatur, and the steps I would need to take to make it happen were regularly occurring conversations. Even though I was young at the time, she never talked to me like a child. Maybe she knew the life I had lived thus far, as well as what was to come and wanted me to be prepared. I had told Stacey my dreams of going to an all-black college, and joining a sorority. I had seen movies and videos of these types of schools and knew I wanted to be a part of that action someday. I loved the way the sororities and fraternities were like family. Seeing this made me want to belong even more. Stacey listened and never looked or acted judgmental. She encouraged all my hopes and dreams, and never once said they sounded silly or impossible. Even on one of my visits to see her when I completely switched things up and spoke *about becoming an actress, she still encouraged me to do what I really had a passion for and wanted to pursue. Even if she didn't really care, and it was all an act, she was doing more in my life than I could say for most people I had come across. It was weird seeing her again after all this time, and even weirder seeing her while not being confined inside the group home. I had been lucky to escape those particular locks, but more were rapidly approaching as we drove off.*

I didn't know exactly where she was taking me and I had been moved around so much that at this point I didn't really care as long as it was away from Wanda. No goodbyes were apparently necessary from Wanda because she wasn't even home when I was picked up and taken away this time. She didn't hit me with any excuses or ask me to come sit on the couch to explain anything to me. She just decided she had more important things to do I assume. I knew goodbyes weren't necessary either, because this would be the last

opportunity she would ever get to throw me out as if I

was just another garbage bag full of trash. Telling Taka

and Sheem bye wasn't necessary either because I knew

I would see them one day soon. Proper goodbyes up to

this point in life weren't something I was accustomed to,

and that was okay because I hated how saying goodbye

made me feel. I hated that a simple goodbye made me

feel like the situation was permanent and not temporary.

That day began and ended like any other day, and

everyone went about with their lives as such, except for

me. I had my few trash bags packed and ready to go.

Time had come once again to start all over.

We traveled to what appeared to be the outskirts of

Decatur. The houses were spaced out and the yards

were huge. The area gave me the feeling of being in the

country even though that wasn't actually the case. We

drove down a long driveway before coming to a stop.

Once out of the car I looked at the next place I would lay my head. Without us even knocking, the side door flew open, and a bubbly and smiling face appeared. I knew my face looked surprised at what I was seeing, so I quickly corrected it. I hadn't been told I was moving this far out, nor that my new foster mom was young and white. She didn't look a day over 30, and would be telling me what I could and couldn't do? She looked pleasant enough, and I didn't get those same feelings I had during my first encounter with Mrs. Rice, but this was still different and something inside me didn't feel right about this situation, but then again nowadays nothing felt right. The lady staring at me didn't look as if she would beat anyone, let alone a child. She actually had one of the sweetest most genuine-looking faces I had ever seen, but I learned over the years that looks and smiles could be deceiving. I definitely planned on doing what I had taught myself early on, and that was to trust no one. I didn't worry about my new foster mom hitting me, because if she raised anything to hit me, she would be in for a rude awakening.

Once we were invited in, I noticed she was carrying a toddler in her arms with a huge smile on his face. She clearly was familiar with taking in black children, because here she stood with one placed on her hip, and one about to move in. Was she trying to prove something by taking in not only one but two of us black foster kids? Was she planning to get more of us? She had to be getting more money or something by taking both of us in. Nope, I wouldn't trust her, even if I didn't have a reason. She might not beat me, but she was definitely after something, had to be.

Amy didn't live alone but shared a home with her elderly mom. I noticed immediately upon moving in that the relationship they shared mimicked the type of relationship I would want with my mom if I had one. They were *always respectful to one another even when they didn't*

agree, and shared laughs often. I think back on my short

time there and can't help but wonder if this was God's

way of briefly exposing me to what a healthy mother and

daughter relationship should look like. As a teenager, and

in that moment, appreciation had taken a backseat in my

mind, and life was still happening all around me. Because

of this all the signs of her being a good person were

ignored. I ignored the way she nurtured and cared for her

toddler foster child. The fact that she helped me buy my

very first car, which allowed me to remain in the same

high school clearly wasn't enough of a sign for me. Her

getting my hair done, buying me a beautiful homecoming

dress, paying for senior pictures out of her own money

wasn't enough either. There were so many other signs

that I should have seen but life had done such a number

on me that I ignored the obvious. I ignored the fact that

she was just trying to do right by helping kids who clearly

needed it. Instead, I repaid her by doubting her

generosity, and by losing my virginity on the floor of the family room while she and her mom were out. The star basketball player of a nearby high school had given me attention and had gotten into my head. I clearly had a type and believed every lie he spat out thinking I was special. He took my innocence on the family room floor, and I allowed it. I would once again lay on the ground bleeding, but for very different reasons this time.

I wanted to believe that a boy could really love me, and this was the way he showed me that he cared about me. I wanted to believe that if I gave him what he wanted, which was that special part of me, he would give me what I needed in return and love me. I would turn out to be wrong on so many levels. Most of the girls that I knew had already lost their virginity, but not me. Where had it gotten me by holding on to it? I reasoned with myself as he lay on top of me. I convinced myself if I gave him what no other man had, he would have to think I was special. I had gotten all these ideas in my head that since he had taken my virginity, we surely would be together now. I had convinced myself of so many things that ultimately were not the case. He would definitely take me to his homecoming that was approaching as his date was what I told myself. The girls would envy me. They would wish that it was them standing arm and arm with him, but nope it would be me and only me. Big wishing and dreaming was what I was doing.

Instead of him taking me to his homecoming and him coming to mine, excuses for why it couldn't happen were all I heard. He had even told me he would be out of town visiting a college as a recruit prospect the weekend of his homecoming and of course I believed him. I found out later that not only was he at homecoming, he was crowned King. He had just chosen to share the experience with someone else. Pretty soon the excuses stopped and so did the calls. I was crushed to say the least, and the sadness and thoughts of the large piece of me that I had handed over to him so freely stayed with me. How could I be this stupid and actually believe what he said? I had always gone by the motto, "trust no one," and I had slipped bad. Was I becoming exactly what Mrs. Rice had destined me to be, a fast little girl that would eventually end up barefoot and pregnant? Thank goodness he knew more about sex than I did and had come prepared with protection. I just hoped the protection worked, and "being fast" didn't come with a baby. I never wanted one of those.

Day after day, Amy attempted to give her all into being a good foster parent in hopes of me becoming a part of their family, and every day I crushed that for her. I didn't know how to build healthy relationships, and now that I had stepped deeper into womanhood, I felt more grown than ever before. Amy ended up receiving the backlash that came with a heart-broken teenage girl, and I soon *would find out that people can only take so much before giving up and throwing in the towel. The feeling that something wasn't right when I moved in wasn't because of Amy, it was because of me. I was the one not right. The lack of trust I had for everyone couldn't be hidden, and because of that, hurting was all I had become accustomed to.*

Within months, that knocking on the door came once again and my time had expired in yet another home. "An unappreciative heart will land you in the streets just as fast as a drug addicted mother," I soon realized. This time I had no one to blame but myself.

Amy's house would be the last foster home I would ever live in. Even though I was unworthy, God would continue to watch over me. For whatever reason, He refused to give up on me even when I gave up on myself. At the time I didn't even think of what was to come as being

God's work. Somewhere in the back of my mind I was still holding onto the notion I was owed something. I should have learned when Aunt Linda was taken away that I wasn't owed anything and nothing was promised, but nope. Eventually though, the time would come when I would have no other choice but to acknowledge that it was no one but God that was continuing to make a way for me and my undeserving ways, but it wouldn't be during this next phase of life.

Own My Own

At 17, no other foster homes wanted to take me in. I was blessed to be able to become a part of a program called ISL (Independent Supportive Living). This program was not offered to all teens my age in care, and because of this a large number of teens aged out of foster care at 18 and went off to survive the best way they could.

Joining this program, however, meant many things for me. I would still be a ward of the state, and technically still a foster child, but I now had the opportunity to live on my own with some restrictions. These restrictions came with a lot of financial help so I couldn't complain too much. There would be rules I would have to follow while in the program, but I knew there were always ways around rules. I would also have to maintain a part-time job to live in the apartment they were setting me up in, but that was no issue for me because I enjoyed working and having my own money.

Having guests over after a certain time wasn't allowed, and I'd better be in school every day or have a darn good reason as to why I wasn't. I hated the sadness I felt being alone and being in school made sure I was never alone. I was told a social worker could stop by at any time of the night or day so to just follow the rules. Saying this was possibly an attempt to stop teens in the program from attempting to break the rules, but I wasn't fooled, and neither were any of the others in the program. The reality was caseworkers were overworked as it was, and there was already never enough of them to do day check-ins, let alone late-night check-ins.

In return for following the rules, my rent and utilities would all be taken care of, as well as a few other expenses. After some time, the part time job would assist me in taking over some of my bills then eventually all of them. I would be living my best life, or so I thought.

I was getting up, going to school every morning, and doing my homework on rare occasions. I felt so independent now that I had my own place and was working that I had even picked up a second job as a hostess at a nearby restaurant. School work was definitely the least of my concerns. The ISL program advised against working more than a certain amount of hours while still in school, but I didn't plan on listening to that. I would need to prepare myself for when I no longer had any assistance. I knew how foster care was, and even though this situation was different, I knew how quickly "situations" were likely to change.

My apartment happened to be located within walking distance of Auntie Linda's home. Living back in the same area was hard for me. Knowing my old home was right down the street made my heart hurt often when I felt alone in my apartment. I wished many days and nights that the apartment was all a dream and Aunt Linda was still alive for me to finish out my senior year in our home. This, however, would remain a wish that would never come true.

Night after night, I would sit alone, becoming more and more depressed, sulking in my situation and life. I didn't have a reason to be depressed, I often thought, but here I was sad all the time. My friends thought I had it made, but everything in me wanted a parent telling me what I could and couldn't do. I would prefer to have to sneak out at night, not just walk out the front door. I wanted my cute girlish bedroom back in Aunt Linda's house, not a mattress and box spring lined up against a wall in a one-bedroom, undecorated apartment. I didn't want to have to go grocery shopping to buy food to have in my fridge to eat. I would prefer to raid my parents' fridge like all my friends did when they wanted to eat. Life can be a funny thing, because while I thought my friends had it made, they were thinking I had it made. I thought I wanted this life, but here I was missing what came with being a child. Auntie Linda, Nana, and even Amy were missed now more than ever before.

I soon became dependent on my friends being around. When no one was around and my little apartment was silent with nothing but my box TV placed on a black milk crate on the ground, I became more lost in my own head with thoughts of my past that was the reason I was now in this situation.

I never wanted anyone to know the pain I was feeling, so I walked around with a smile on my face at all times, being the funny man of our group and the life of the party. I cracked jokes, always wanting those around me to never feel what I felt on the inside every day of my life.

Life wasn't standing still, and neither were my feelings. I silently became more and more depressed, now crying to the bathroom mirror in my tiny apartment, ashamed to talk to anyone, believing I would look weak.

I graduated high school at my lowest point. On a day that should have been one of the happiest days of my life, I forced a smile on my face and walked across the stage with no one in attendance to see me. My friends and classmates that were graduating and their families were the only ones to cheer me on as I walked the stage to accept my diploma. Due to a tornado watch that occurred a couple hours before graduation, I didn't mind that no one was probably coming. It wasn't until I saw the gymnasium still jam-packed with families and friends that hadn't let the tornado stop them from their loved ones' special day, that I realized once again just how unimportant I was in the world to most people. It hurt me to know if Aunt Linda was alive, she would be front and center screaming at the top of her lungs, proud of my

accomplishment, even if she was alone.

Wanda walked into graduation as I walked out. I was

surprised she made an appearance at all but here she

was. She hadn't made it to see me walk across the stage

or watch me get the scholarship I received that night, but

at least here she was. Maybe she wasn't so bad after all.

A New City

Something had to give was all I could think as I headed to the corn dog stand to work yet another 8-hour shift. I didn't mind working, but thoughts of where my future stood if I stayed started to concern me. Since I had graduated, I was working a lot more hours, knowing my time in the ISL program was rapidly approaching. Rumor was that once you turned 18 you were dropped from the program, and I was officially that. The big dreams I had of becoming a teacher, college life, and sorority life would all have to be put on the back burner for now. I had real life issues to figure out. Money was needed now, and not in the 4 to 5 years it would take to obtain a degree.

Even though I was not quite sure where my life was headed, I knew that dipping corn dogs in grease couldn't be it for me. High school friendships had fizzled off since graduation and my old crew were all doing their own *things. We had talked over the years about relocating out of Decatur. Chicago, St. Louis, and Atlanta had all been mentioned. Kindle at the time had no plans of leaving Decatur and was one of the only friends that I still hung out with on a regular basis.*

Crystal moved to St. Louis to become a flight attendant, which intrigued me, only I was absolutely terrified to fly. I had never been on a plane before in my life but was still curious about her new life and job. I had heard she was flying all over and had her own place and was doing great in St. Louis. I wanted to see different parts of the world, and this sounded like the perfect opportunity. I decided, scared or not, I wanted in on the action. I was excited to find out I met all the necessary requirements, and quickly applied.

When the call came, I traveled to STL and interviewed with TWE airlines. I was offered the job before my interview had ended and told I would just need to wait for my background check to come back. The ISL program was extremely proud of the initiative I was taking. The program decided instead of pushing me to the streets at 18, they would let me remain until I was 21. This would be another blessing from God that I would later look back on and think of how I was so undeserving. The majority of youth in care would never have this opportunity, and the only condition that I was given was to continue down the right path.

A terrified 19-year-old girl traveled to a new city with her caseworker driving the way in hopes of finding an apartment in the largest city she had ever been in. Needless to say, I was beyond terrified. We looked for an apartment in one day because the program couldn't afford to pay for us to stay overnight. Thankfully we found what I hoped would be my future apartment after hours of searching. We then headed back to Decatur with *uncertainty and excitement taking over me all at once. Could I survive in a new place? Was I making the right choice by leaving the only place I ever knew? Either way there was no turning back now, although I considered it several times.*

Within a month of being approved for my apartment, I was on the road to start my next journey in life. Once settled into STL, I prayed things would improve and the thoughts that continuously invaded my mind to end it all would go away. It might take some adjustment time, I told myself, but the depression, anger, sadness, and anxiety would have to go away now. A new setting and city was just what I convinced myself I needed.

It wouldn't take long for me to figure out that Decatur wasn't the issue, Wanda wasn't even the issue, but that I had issues that ran way deeper than what my mind could catch up to comprehending. The fact that I never talked to anyone about my feelings of abandonment, the abuse I endured from Mrs. Rice, or the depression I was dealing with on a daily basis began to hurt me in ways that I wouldn't understand until I was well into womanhood, and completely broken down to nothing. That part of my life will be told a little later in my story, but for now, know that when you feel you are down to nothing, God is always up to something.

I kicked butt in my flight attendant training class. As people were being dropped from training every day for failing a single test, I continued to study hard, knowing I had no backup option or anyone to turn to if this didn't work out. Failure was not an option, so week after week and test after test I gave it all I had. Within six weeks I had earned my flight wings, and the hands-on in-flight training was ready to begin. During my interview process I had never divulged that I had never flown before nor had I ever stepped foot inside an airplane or airport for *that matter. Letting them know that I was completely terrified of heights I knew would immediately be a deal breaker as well. I kept all this information to myself as a job I was surely not qualified to have was offered to me.*

I would soon have to become the actor I once dreamed of being and put on the best show of my life to not look completely terrified, sitting on a plane about to take off for my very first time.

I sat in the seat that had been reserved just for me, watching the flight attendant prep for the flight. Once the flight was boarded, I watched how she gracefully pointed out the exit signs, and what to do in case of an emergency evacuation as if she had done it a thousand times before. I wasn't sure if I would ever be as good as she was but planned on giving it my all. I remained calm until she began to go over what to do in case of a water evacuation. My anxiety immediately started to kick in and

I could feel the sweat starting to form on my forehead. Realizing on top of everything else that if the plane went down over water, I couldn't swim only made things worse. I turned my head to not be seen and closed my eyes. I knew all I could do now was say a prayer. Once the 30-seater jet began to back away from the gate, I began to question every choice I had made up to this point in my life. It was too late now because the doors were closed, and take-off time was quickly approaching. I was now officially confined in the tiny space of the plane for the next hour. There was no turning back, but I knew I had definitely made the biggest mistake thinking becoming a flight attendant was the next best move after corn dogs.

I made my first training flight praying the whole time, but I made it, and alive. I knew what was to come next and definitely wasn't ready for it. Within the next couple of days, the call and the time had come. I was officially on the schedule to fly alone, and I knew that would be completely different. I would have no one to rely on, as I would be the only flight attendant working the flight. I woke up the morning of debating whether to quit or not, but realized if I quit, I would have no money, no clue of what to do next, and would have wasted six weeks of my life giving my all in training. Deciding that not going wasn't an option, I loaded my overnight bag for my trip and headed to the airport. Airport life was a lot different than the initial tour we had taken while in training. I felt as though a training was needed on how to maneuver through Lambert Airport in itself. I was definitely still a small-town girl caught up in big city living. The airport was busy with crew members and passengers moving about not slowing down to even take a breath. I, on the other hand, looked like a deer in headlights, while everyone else moved about checking to see gates for departures. I stood trying to figure out what I needed to do first, let alone next.

"You need help?" I turned around to see a pleasant, middle-aged female flight attendant staring back at me.

"Yes, please, I'm so lost," I answered with a smile. All the boards and military times along with flight and plane information was too much for me to process on my first day. We had gone over it in training but being in on the action was different.

"Let me see your itinerary for your trip," she asked. Once I had shown her, she was able to show me how to read the screens to find my plane. I was grateful she was there to help, otherwise I'm not sure how long I would have stared helplessly at the screen; but now I was headed across the ramp, and to my plane. The plane I was working wasn't parked far, but to my surprise it had propellers. We had trained on a grounded one but most of the training was put towards the jets that the airline *was transitioning into. Having low seniority meant my first flight alone was going to be propeller style.*

The plane was even smaller than the jet I had done my initial training on. As much as the size of the plane made me want to turn back, I knew that I couldn't now that the pilot and co-pilot were looking at me. I introduced myself to both as I began to do my prep that needed to be completed before the passengers boarded. The pilot informed me that we would encounter bad weather during the short flight, and an inflight beverage service would not be needed. One less thing I have to do and more time to pray, I thought as the 15 passengers came walking across the ramp heading straight towards my small plane. Once I had greeted them one by one, and they were all settled in and the manifest was checked and ready to go, I pulled the cabin door shut and locked it. I was immediately shook as to what was about to happen. I knew I had no choice but to pull it together and quickly, and that's exactly what I did. I took several deep breaths before facing the crowd that now had all eyes on me. Ready or not, this flight was going to take off and I needed to prepare everyone, including myself. Knowing what I had to do, I gave the widest smile I could force on my face and pointed out how to follow the lighting in the floor to the nearest exit in case of an emergency. I began to point out the other safety features of the plane, as well as advise the passengers on how to use their seatbelt and inflate their life vest in the event of a water evacuation, while praying we would never have to use it. Right about the time I finished, the pilot rang the chime throughout the plane that signaled I needed to take my seat and prepare for takeoff.

Takeoff propeller-style was a lot rougher than being on the jet. While the jet glided into the sky, I could hear the propellers going at full speed as the small plane seemed to give its all climbing to the altitude that the pilots *needed it to be at. Once we had reached the desired altitude the pilot's voice came over the intercom. He introduced himself and his copilot before informing everyone that bad weather would be approaching soon and everyone needed to be prepared to stay in their seats for the duration of the short flight.*

What came next for me was nothing short of what I had seen in movies, where you are pretty sure the plane is about to crash and there will be no survivors. If there are survivors after the crash, the plane would probably be in an area where it couldn't be found, or with my luck, in water and everyone would still die anyway.

The skies all around us grew a dark that looked shades darker when you were actually in the clouds instead of on the ground. The rain and lightning began hitting the plane as if both were giving the plane the beating of its life. The small aircraft began jerking back and forth as I assume the pilots were working hard to keep it under control. I sat still and afraid, focused and thinking about everything from the propellers to death. I knew that in order for us to stay in the sky those propellers needed to keep turning. If they didn't keep turning, death was approaching, and I wasn't ready for that either. As I was focused on everything else the passengers were now all looking back focusing on me. Questions began to pour in as if I was in the cockpit making the decisions. I wanted to tell all of them "I know as much as you all do, and this is my first flight ever alone, so just leave me be and let me pray." Instead, I smiled and gave them the reassurance they were looking for, that I, myself, didn't even have.

"It's going to be okay; we should be landing in about 30 minutes." Once I had reassured them as best I could, I went into my head space and began to pray even more as the lightning looked more intense than it had a few moments earlier. "Dear God please help us, please give

the pilots the ability to keep the plane up and land safely,"

was my prayer. This was definitely not how I saw my life

coming to an end. As much as I had prayed for God to

just take my life in the past, this was a time I remember

praying to him to save it.

"Make sure your seatbelts are securely fastened, it will be

a rough landing," the pilot informed us as we inched

closer to the airport. The rain was still beating down on

the plane as the pilots began to descend into the city.

Everyone sat quietly gripping what they could to prepare

themselves for whatever was to come. I could see land

getting closer, and the landing gear coming out which

brought me some peace, but also had me tugging at my

own seatbelt to make sure it was securely fastened. The

landing onto the runway was so hard it made us all jump

and gasp in our seats. The plane began to slow and then

glide the remainder of the way until we were safely

landed. The passengers were so excited to be on the

ground that cheers were being given to the pilot and co-pilot for their efforts. God had heard my prayers and we didn't die that night but once this two-day trip was over, my career as a flight attendant definitely would be too. I just prayed I would last one more day.

Broken Love

The way my anxiety was set up, leaving the friendly skies
was the best thing for me and I knew it. The problem was
that I needed a replacement job, and I needed it now. I
could never tell my caseworker I had quit my job and risk
being dropped from the program, especially now.
Instead, I found a part time job in the mall to hold me
over, and said nothing. I always felt the desire to do work
in which I felt I was serving out my purpose, but since I
wasn't completely sure what my purpose was in life, the
mall would have to do for now. I worked part-time and
full-time jobs in a clothing and jewelry store until another
airline called me to come in and interview for a position
as a gate agent. Although I wasn't excited about being in
the skies, I had enjoyed the fast-moving pace of the
airport once I knew how to navigate throughout it. A job
at the airport would be exactly what I needed for now to

keep me busy, as long as my feet were able to stay
planted on land.

I killed the job interview, and my next step was to set out
for Dallas to attend a two-week training. I had nothing
holding me back and was excited to learn new things
about the airline industry. Seeing a new city in the
process was a plus. I would have to fly to Dallas but had
convinced myself I could handle a flight now and then,
just never several flights every day. As long as I could
close my eyes and pray most of the flight, I would be just
fine. Being in Dallas allowed me to see that there was
much more to life than just St. Louis, the same way St.
Louis had shown me there was more outside of Decatur
to be seen. I just had to work on embracing change and
stop letting fear and doubt hold me back.

Training was just as demanding as flight attendant training, but I passed and was now ready to begin my new position back in St. Louis as a gate agent.

I arrived back ready to work and even more ready to make some real money. I had been praying to God a lot, asking for my finances to get in order, and even more for him to send a husband my way. I was willing to take whichever came first. I knew I should focus on work, but loneliness was becoming a friend whose company I didn't enjoy. I had grown tired of not having anyone, and hoped God wasn't too busy to hear me.

He must have been listening because I hadn't been working long before I was approached by Sean. Sean worked for the same airline but as a ramp agent, and was 8 years older than me. He wasn't the type of guy I would normally be attracted to, but he was kind and gentle, and way more mature than other guys in my past. The fact that he had beautiful hazel eyes helped with the fact he was short. I preferred a taller man but could look past that for now. His Will Smith ears that poked straight from his head were something else I wasn't a fan of, but his beautiful caramel complexion allowed me to look past those too. If nothing else, he had eyes for me, and not just the other way around. We began to talk and get to know one another. Before I knew it, we were spending most of our time together between work and home, becoming good friends. The relationship worked well for me because I wasn't ready for more than a friendship with him. I knew God was working on my husband, and I planned to be ready whenever he showed up.

"Girl, let's get out and do something," Kindle said, over the phone, trying to convince me to get out of bed and go out with her. I had finally talked her into moving to STL and she was having the time of her life. She was meeting new people and doing some promotional modeling. I had

even gotten her on at the airport with me, and she couldn't be happier with her move. She knew I wasn't the biggest fan of clubbing, but tonight I had the urge to get out and go to a party that was being advertised on the radio. We arrived late to the college party, and the crowd was slim which was perfect for me because I hated large crowds. I had put on my cute clubbing outfit which meant little was left to the imagination, and I was ready to dance the night away no matter the size of the crowd. As Kindle and I began to dance, a handsome man with girls flocking to his every move appeared off in the distance. I couldn't help but stop dancing and stare because I had never seen a man so intriguing with no words ever spoken. The way he dressed and the way he carried himself was a clear sign he wasn't a college boy. Once our eyes connected, I told myself this was it. God must have sent our paths to cross because physically he had everything on my want list. He was tall, light-skinned, bearded, and had a fresh fade that made every wave in his head stand out. I found out that not only was he in attendance at the party, but he was the one throwing it. I knew he had to be much older than I was, but I had no plans of walking away before names and numbers were exchanged. What I didn't know was that a simple exchange of numbers was going to bring about a strong lesson for a simple-minded young girl that thought wants should outweigh needs.

Let's get back to Sean though. He was quiet and reserved which was way different from my personality. He wasn't into attire such as clothes and shoes and kept a low profile. He valued his family and friends and should have been the poster boy for what a person looks like that treats others as they themselves would want to be treated. He didn't go to clubs, or any type of party for that matter, and his definition of a good time was cooking food and watching movies. As crazy as it was, this was actually my definition of a good time too, but because I wasn't physically into him, or so I assumed was the issue, like I was Avery the club promoter, real chances weren't even given to him. I wanted Sean to change. I wanted him to be this adventurous person that even I wasn't. I enjoyed staying in and watching movies, but for some reason nothing he did was ever good enough for me. He worked hard, often going into the airport 7 days a week working doubles from 6am to 11pm. As we hung out more, he became that positive male figure that also possessed a nurturing and loving side that I never knew men had. He was different in a way that was new to me, but because the attraction wasn't there, I refused to let him distract me from the husband God had for me.

The first time Avery responded to my message, I lit up like a Christmas tree. We didn't have much to talk about that text or any of the others that followed but that was okay, I told myself. I knew he was a very busy man, so that had to be the reason. He was not only throwing parties but getting ready to open his own club. He was

also a comedian by night and worked 9-to-5 by day.

I was in denial and chose not to acknowledge that what

Avery wanted from me was not what I wanted from him.

The text every couple of weeks wasn't because he was

just that busy, but because that was as much as he cared

to talk to me. The late nights were for one thing and one

thing only. Once he had gotten what he wanted he

jokingly excused himself and left the tiny apartment that I

had now moved into. I was officially 21 and paying rent

completely on my own as a "grown" woman. This meant I

would no longer live in the beautiful garden style

apartment that ISL had set me up in, but something that I

could afford independently, along with all the utilities.

Sadly, what I could afford was located in a not-so-safe

side of town.

Even though Avery might not want me now, he would eventually, and when he did, I would be right there. Once again, I was fooling myself. I wasn't the first or the last girl that he would invite into his home. He hadn't told me that he was looking for anything more with me, and was showing me just that, but he too had received that special part of me, so there had to be more. Yes, still young, naive, and broken was definitely what I was, and stupidity and Avery would make me pay for it the hard way.

Sean and I continued our friendship which eventually grew into more. It wasn't that I necessarily wanted more, but he was such a great guy I figured why not when he asked me to be his girl. Even though I was falling in what I believed to be love with someone else, I decided to commit to Sean knowing I wasn't mentally fully invested. The promoter, like most men, grew tired, and just like that even the every-few-weeks texts stopped.

Sean and I officially became a couple even as the devil played with my thoughts. Avery wouldn't escape them nor my dreams and within a little over a year, Sean and I went to the courthouse and were married. I knew Sean loved me with all his heart and would do anything for me. Even though my heart wasn't 100 percent invested I figured it would get there. Sean never switched up on me, and I never grew concerned like I had in other relationships that he was cheating on me, so why didn't I love him? What was wrong with me? I knew I was broken but if I was capable of "loving Avery", why couldn't I feel that way towards a man that was willing to give me the world. Was I just stupid? Was God trying to tell me something?

I knew what I needed to do. I needed to let Avery know exactly how I felt. If he didn't feel the same, then just maybe Sean could finally have all of me, and I could finally appreciate the good man he was. I sat down at our *home computer and typed a four-page letter confessing my love to a man that didn't want me then and definitely wouldn't after reading a love letter that I'm sure left me looking weak and vulnerable. I then thought it would be smart to deliver it to him at his home and leave. I continued making one bad move after another. My four-page letter made no difference to him and I'm sure after it was read, if it was read, it was then thrown somewhere, and his life continued on.*

My life, on the other hand, continued spiraling out of control once Sean read the saved letter addressed to another man. I told Sean that I wasn't happy in our marriage several times and it wasn't his fault, but never did he imagine just how unhappy I was. I waited for him to blow up at me and throw me out of the house, but he never did. Instead, he agreed to a divorce that I knew he didn't really want. He then helped me find a place of my own and even furnished it. He talked to me day in and day out when I needed to, even as he was hurting from my mistakes, he never left my side. When I would ask Sean if I made a mistake leaving, he assured me I had done what was best and I needed to find my happiness. I'm sure he probably was thinking I needed to find myself a therapist, but he never said it out loud or placed blame on me even when I knew I deserved it.

At this point in my life, I wasn't even sure how to be happy. If Sean couldn't make me happy, then who could? He had poured all the love he had into me, and I had been too broken to appreciate it. Just like that, my ungrateful heart had once again landed me alone and even more depressed in a situation I had ultimately created. I had told God what I wanted, and later in life I would realize he delivered me exactly what I needed. I was blind and not ready to receive the blessings he had in store for me, and because of that I ultimately walked away with what I would discover later was a lesson learned about prayer. "An unready heart is a prayer said

in vain."

Blood Sisters

This part of my journey is one that still saddens me to talk and think about to this day, but a very important part of my life that I couldn't choose to ignore. As I stated in the beginning, my whole purpose in life and this book is to do my part where I can in breaking cycles. If telling intimate parts of my life can help anyone, then it is worth reliving to put into words and onto paper. When we as individuals and families experience trauma and choose not to deal with the past, the pain experienced will continue to haunt us, and hurt those we love in the most unimaginable ways. Not dealing with trauma left me broken and without the sister that I had craved all my life.

When my sister entered my life, I assumed she was there to stay, I thought she would heal a piece of me that had been missing for so long. I think in some ways she thought I could do the same for her, but this would turn *out not to be the case. The saying that, "Hurt people hurt people," can be true when those hurting never seek what is needed to help heal their pain. I would learn that I couldn't heal her open wounds, and she couldn't heal mine. We both had some of the same battle scars that hadn't ever been tended to. This would cause internal damage to us both. Seeking help and healing ourselves was a step that neither of us had chosen to take. I would eventually learn that a person has to want to find healing for themselves or there is nothing that anyone else can do, and most times that's the hardest lesson anyone can learn. I would learn this lesson a little too late, and my sister and I would meet only to drift further apart until drifting was no longer a choice.*

My cell phone was once again ringing, as I attempted to clean up around the house. During the time that my sister and I first connected was during the same time that Sean and I were disconnecting, if you can call it that, and were planning my move. I was dealing with way too much and in need of a clear head from my own self-induced drama. The number was one I didn't recognize, and for a moment I debated answering, but did so anyway.

"Hi, is this Dovia?"

"Yes," I replied. The caller went on to remind me of paperwork that I had filled out searching for a sibling some time back. I listened, confused at first, until it dawned on me that right before I exited the ISL program, my caseworker had told me of a program for former foster kids. The program allowed them to search for one biological sibling free of charge. She had filled out the paperwork for me and I had forgotten about it expecting nothing to come from it. On the paperwork, I had chosen to look for one of my sisters. I had chosen her because I had always wanted a sister, and because she was a twin. I knew that if I found her, I could potentially find my *brother as well if they hadn't been split up. Over the years, rumors had circulated that they had been adopted by a family in Chicago so there was hope they were still together. I couldn't be sure that any of this information was true, but decided it was the best information I had, and better that than nothing.*

"Hello, are you still there?" the voice on the other end was asking.

"Sorry, yes, I'm still here," I quickly responded, being snapped out of my thoughts.

"I have the number here for your sister's adoptive mom, if you would like to take it down." Once I had written down the number, I thanked her and hung up. I got off the phone not really knowing how to feel. I never expected that she would be located, and potentially be a phone call away. I guess somewhere in my head I thought if the call

ever came it would be to say that she couldn't be found, and life as I had been living it would go on. This, however, was not the case. In my hand I was holding the number that could possibly lead my brother and sister into my life. I had been blessed with Starsky, Taka, and Sheem, but had always yearned for a bigger family, and now this could possibly become a reality. Tears began to flow as I quietly cried. Those cries grew louder and harder. I wasn't crying because I was sad, but because once again a new opportunity was presenting itself. God was going to allow me to have what I had dreamed of for so long.

Excitement and fear took over as I held the future in my hand. What if they didn't like me, or didn't want to see me? They had been living the privileged life of being adopted, and we had to be completely different. My brain started to do what it normally did, which was to go into overdrive, thinking about all the negative possibilities that could come from one phone number. I knew if I didn't call soon, I just might talk myself out of ever calling.

A couple of days later I sat on the living room couch and gathered up the courage I needed to finally make the call. A sweet, older voice came through the receiver after a few rings.

"Hi my name is Dovia, and…"

"I was waiting on your call," she interrupted me very softly to say. My sibling's mom began to tell me that she had been contacted by the agency and had agreed that it was okay for me to contact her first. In the short phone call exchange between us, she told me that my brother still lived at home, and my sister was attending an HBCU in Alabama. That alone completely shocked me. She was actually living out the dreams I had for myself. This made me even more excited to meet her. Her mom went on to

tell me that she would talk to her and share my phone
number. My sister apparently had known she had other
brothers and sisters, and just like me had dreamed of
one day meeting them.

Within a day my phone was ringing with a number I just
knew had to belong to my sister. Sure enough, a high-
pitched voice greeted me from the other end. Her name
was different from the information I had, but I knew it was
her. She began to tell me that after being adopted their
names were changed from the birth names originally
given to them and changed to Michelle and Michael, but
that she wore her biological name with her every day as
a tattoo and reminder of who she was. We continued
talking as if we had known each other all our lives. We
talked about how she and our brother had been adopted
a few years after Starsky and I had gone into foster care.
Through our conversation, I learned Wanda at one time
had custody of them, and just like Starsky and I, she

decided another family was better suited to raise them. Michelle told me her family now lived in Nashville instead of Chicago and had been for years. I grew even more excited knowing that Nashville was less than a 5-hour drive away from St. Louis. I was floored when she told me that she was finishing up her undergraduate degree in special education and had plans to become a teacher while getting her masters then her doctorate in education. God had to be bringing us together for a reason, and I knew that whatever was to come could only be for good.

Thanksgiving arrived and I stopped off in Decatur to pick up Starsky before we made our first ever trip to Nashville. Starsky didn't appear nervous at all, but my thoughts were everywhere as we drove down the highway. We were greeted by Michelle at the door with genuine smiles and hugs. Her beauty immediately had me in complete awe. She was stunning on so many levels. Michelle was biracial and drop-dead gorgeous. She had the beautiful light skin that I had prayed and cried in the mirror for on so many days and nights. Her hair flowed to her shoulders with no assistance from a relaxer or a hot comb like I was used to, and her petite, short frame made me smile because I had always thought I was short, and here she was not standing even 5 feet tall while Michael stood at least 6 feet. When I looked at her, I saw a better, more put-together version of myself. I immediately felt love for my sister and a bond was formed as if it had always been there, just waiting for us to unite.

Michelle and I shared many qualities while Starsky and Michael reminded me so much of one another that it was uncanny. They both shared a love for bowling and were great at it. Even though neither of them had ever possessed a driver's license, and never would, neither had an issue with getting where they needed to go (smooth talkers). They both had a disability that they never let hold them back. That Thanksgiving I noticed that not only were we all siblings, but we were all *survivors of situations and circumstances that we hadn't*

asked to be placed in.

Like everything in life, with the good comes the bad, and

the ugly. Let's just say the bad came veering its head

around the corner in the years that followed with an ugly

vengeance.

The Ugly Truth

Things were great between Michelle and me. The distance apart didn't keep us from talking every day. When either of us needed to vent, the other sister was right there on the other end of the receiver listening and giving advice. Life for both of us was continuously changing, but we continued to strengthen the sisterly bond we never had before. I was going through my struggles within myself with my soon to be ex-husband at the time, and through our many conversations I would learn my sister wasn't living the life I assumed a gorgeous, educated, adopted girl would be.

Homecoming was rapidly approaching in Alabama, and we had decided to plan my first trip there. Excitement could not have even begun to describe how I felt about the trip. It would be the first time I would attend an HBCU, get to see her interactions with her sorority sisters, and *experience a life that I had dreamed of for myself. While in Alabama, I got more than a glimpse into the college life I wanted, but other not so good characteristics that we both shared as well. I had married a man 10 years older than me trying to fill a void, and here she was a mere college student, married for a second time trying to fill what I can only assume was a void as well.*

As we prepared to go to the homecoming basketball game, I saw Michelle for the first time in a light unlike anything I had seen or heard from her. She was always so sweet and gentle, but this day would show a side of her I had never encountered. A great day ended with her and her husband not only throwing out harsh names at one another back and forth but also punches, mainly from her. When all was said and done, all I knew to do was tell her it would be okay like I had heard so many times before. I didn't know if she would be, but I now knew why people had told me those same words so many times before, so here I stood tossing those same words around.

I didn't know what angered her the way it did, but I knew it had to be more than their disagreement that I had witnessed. I told her she could do better than him which I truly believed, but I also knew she needed psychological help just as I did. Trying to tell those you love that help is needed can be a conversation that most of us are afraid to have, including myself at that moment. I thought if I told her how I felt, I would lose her again, so I chose to keep that to myself, only hurting us both in the long run.

Because my pain didn't come out in an aggressive manner, it hadn't dawned on me that we carried some of the same hurt, only we expressed the pain differently. I expressed myself by keeping my hurt and pain bottled up and blocking anyone that meant any good in my life out as soon as one thing didn't go the way I expected it to. I walked away from issue after issue, choosing not to address them, which made me no better. I would realize in the years to come that the demons we were trying to ignore were refusing to stay hidden any longer.

That day, instead of a more put-together version of me, I saw myself in Michelle. She didn't want to be the way she was nor carry her baggage around any more than I did. Just as the depression was and had eaten away at me for years, it was doing the same to her. Looking at my sister that day I saw that everything that glitters isn't always gold. All the things that I had prayed to have— from the light skin, to wanting to be adopted, the flawless hair, skin, and even the college education—weren't making her happy. I knew that day that my happiness would never be found by changing my outer appearance. I needed to look deeper inside of myself, but I wasn't sure where to even begin.

Over the next 10 years our relationship or the lack thereof suffered. There were moments of extreme highs and even more moments of extreme lows. We rarely argued with one another and that was because choosing to walk away was what we were used to when dealing with the same sex. Communication was neither of our strong points, and because of this, years would go by after a misunderstanding with no communication. Our final misunderstanding in 2018 left us with no more words for one another, and ultimately was the end of any type of relationship we would ever have. The failure of our sisterhood was another case and example of a broken family, and generational curses. It became clearer than ever to see what happens when hurt becomes all you know, and ending that cycle becomes something that can't be undone alone.

After every encounter where we would have a falling out for whatever silly reason, I shed tears. After more than 10 years of tears off and on, I finally had no more tears left to shed. Years and years of tears throughout my life taught me that with every step of my journey a lesson was learned even if I couldn't see it at that moment. God was right there, seeing and hearing me even in my lowest moments such as losing my sister, just waiting for me to get out of my own way.

"We look for others to inspire us, not realizing you yourself are an inspiration in someone's eyes. Stop seeking affirmation from others to validate what you already know." ~Dovia~

Part 3

Up to this point the feeling of no control consumed me. I had no control over when the depression would come crashing in and leave me for days and even weeks not wanting to move or talk to anyone. I felt I had no control over my thoughts or feeling that I needed love from a man to end my depression, and even still no control over when he was coming, if at all. I had no control over my past, and now my present continued barreling out of control. Feeling like I had no control made me want control even more. This feeling left me seeking one relationship after another as each failed. I knew most of the time the relationships were undeserving of me and my time, but it was better than being alone. Time after time I somehow convinced myself that this one had potential without even utilizing my own.

In part 3 of my book and my life, I began to realize that while there were so many things out of my control, God had prepared me over the years with the necessary tools to finally take control of the things that were in my control. It wouldn't be easy but in this next journey of life, I would finally realize who really had control over everyone and everything, and it wasn't man at all. God would show me that if I just stepped aside and out of my own way, he was ready to redeem me and my life in ways greater than what my vision could see, or mind could ever imagine. Redemption was ready and waiting for me but not before the devil took me through hell and back first.

"In this Life you will be dealt some unknown cards, but ultimately how you play them will determine the outcome of the game." ~Dovia~

Trent

Life had definitely been dealing me crappy hands up to this point, and the depression was doing a number on my emotions daily. I was waking every day telling myself to let this not be the day I gave in to the negative feelings and thoughts. I knew somehow and some way I needed to keep pushing but it was getting harder and harder every day. The sadness had gotten to the point where it had become unbearable most days. My belief in God and his words that told me trouble doesn't always last were all I had to lean on, but deep inside I felt my breaking point was nearing. I had suffered more than enough and just prayed the good days would soon start to outweigh the bad days.

Speaking my mind had gotten me fired for the first and only time in my life from the airport and I was now following what I believed was my purpose in life. Helping individuals that were unable to do so for themselves made me feel needed and wanted, and I was darn good at it. My new profession didn't pay much hourly, but I knew like always I would figure it out. Working in a field that had a high turnover rate was beneficial for those not intimidated by the work. Overtime was always available any time I might want it or need it, and the need came very often. I never looked down on myself for having to bathe or wipe a disabled person. I was no better than the individuals I supported and I became more humbled the longer I worked. I always carried the thought on days I didn't want to go in that at any time this could be me. If ever in the situation, I could only pray a caring person would do the same for me. I had heard throughout the years that several of my siblings that my mom gave up were disabled, and I was determined to do my job as if I was taking care of my own blood. The truth was I could have been and never even know it.

While I started out only making $8.50 an hour in 2002, with overtime and a lot of hard work, God saw fit to make a way for me to buy my first dream home, and a new vehicle, all within months of each other. Things were looking up, and there was no time to wallow in my depression. Working 16 hours a day didn't give me much time for anything else, especially when there were people in the world that had issues that surpassed mine. I knew I needed to be strong so that every day I could do my best, and that's exactly what I did. My schedule became: wake up, go to work, come home, go to bed, and then start the process all over again the next day. Working long days helped to keep my mind out of that dark place, at least for a short time. Being able to make others smile, even when I couldn't, would have to be enough for now.

This Tuesday was like any other Tuesday night, except surprisingly, I was only on the schedule to work the morning shift. Kindle and I had decided to go and have some drinks at one of the local nightclubs in the city. (Bet you can't guess who that club belonged to.) With it being a weekday, I knew it shouldn't be too crowded which meant no waiting in long lines. We would be able to drink in peace and go home. After some drinks, dancing, and some laughs, we headed home.

"Hey there, wait up," voices could be heard saying behind us. As we continued to walk across the street to the car the voices grew louder until they were right on us. Kindle and I both turned around to see who felt the need to keep talking and walking behind us even as we gave them none of our attention. We had known that it must be someone that wanted one of our numbers, but the way some of the STL men were set up, it was always safer to just keep walking.

"What's the rush?" I turned around, ready with about five lies in my head that I would tell him if it was me and not

Kindle that he wanted to talk to. Instead, I was standing face to face with a handsome man. The men normally went for Kindle, being that she had legs that went on for days, but the way he smiled at me, I knew I was the chosen one. We exchanged numbers after a short conversation and I want to say the rest is history, but of course that would be too simple to be my life.

The handsome man's name was Trent, and he called the very next day. We decided to meet for lunch in the upcoming days. He was everything a girl could wish for. After one lunch we became inseparable. We enjoyed laughing together and getting out to do things around the city. I wasn't sure if he was the man in my prayers, but I enjoyed how I felt being with him. Hopefully he would be my Prince Charming and turn all my sadness into happiness.

It wouldn't take long before the fantasy was over and Trent was revealing to me over a game of bowling that he currently had not only one woman pregnant at the time, but two. I'm not sure what made him think delivering that news to me with a bowling ball in my hand was a good idea, but he did. Even with the news he delivered, Trent was so smooth with his lies that I believed every word he said about the women meaning nothing. My feelings were too deeply invested to give up now. I knew I hadn't planned on having any children of my own, but I loved kids, so why not step in and help Trent with the two he had on the way.

Trent's new bundles of joy came within the next 4 months of our fresh relationship. The babies were awesome and I loved holding them, changing, feeding, and just being there with them and Trent, but of course, life wasn't giving me my happily ever after that easy. Trent's oldest son's mother had other plans, and decided right off that *she didn't like me, and had no problem expressing that. His other son's mother I knew was still in love with him even though Trent denied it often. I was no fool, and I knew how women acted when in love with a man. Both situations bothered me, and I probably should have walked away, but I refused to give up on this relationship too. I had lost my marriage, lost boyfriends, I didn't want to lose what I thought was meant for me and Trent. My work and Trent seemed to be the only things that helped my mind stay free of my own issues, but my life was about to come down fast and hard all around me. The truths I was trying to ignore about Trent were about to quickly come to the light.*

"Trent, I see the emails, just be honest and admit that she is still in love with you, and you two are messing around." Trent and I had been together for close to four years, and in all that time something told me that he and his youngest child's mother had something going on

during different parts of our relationship. I could never prove it until now, but he needed to help me understand and quickly what was going on with the flirtatious emails I had read. Trent was standing in front of me looking confused as I told him I had seen the emails on his computer that he had left open. Even with the proof staring him in the eyes, Trent was refusing to accept responsibility for anything. He repeated over and over like always, that it was nothing.

"Nothing doesn't sound like this email," I was now screaming at the top of my lungs. "Get out, get out and take your stuff with you." I didn't know if I really meant the words coming out of my mouth, but I felt used and taken advantage of, like I had my whole life. The fact that Trent was lying after all these years meant I wasn't even worth the simple truth, and that alone made me feel defeated and betrayed. I now felt more alone than ever before.

"Get out, get out," I screamed over and over again as Trent moved from the closet to the bed throwing clothes and shoes into trash bags. He was throwing items into trash bags but unlike me in the past he had somewhere he could go. I became even more hurt and angered looking at the now-filled bags. At moments, I wanted him to move faster and get out with those bags, and at the same time I wanted him to convince and tell me that what I saw on his computer was not what I had thought at all. Instead of convincing me of anything he continued moving at a pace that irritated me more and more. He packed bag after bag, not uttering one reason as to why he would betray me like this. Once he was done upstairs, he moved to the basement and then the main floor, taking the TV off the wall. Who did he think he was? He had stayed in my home while I asked for nothing, and was sending inappropriate emails, and then still had the nerve to want to take the one thing in the house he had paid for... the TV. My blood was now boiling to a point I

couldn't control. The devil came creeping in on my shoulder saying, "don't allow this, that's your TV," while the God in me was saying, "calm down and take some deep breaths." The devil would win this battle easily. I had gotten to the point of rage I couldn't control, and let Trent know I would call the police before he left with any TV in my home. I only became even more infuriated when he told me to do what I needed to do. I wasn't sure who Trent was anymore, and I definitely hadn't the slightest idea who this woman was that I had become. Had she been inside of me all these years waiting for the right time to come out, or was this a new woman being born? Either way she wasn't nice, or thinking rationally.

Trent finished packing and had made it outside with the TV. I refused to let him make it to his car. I had told myself if I wasn't even worth a 300-dollar TV after all these years, neither of us would have it. It wasn't even really about the TV as much as the principle behind it all.

How dare he. I started grabbing the TV as he attempted to hold onto it tightly. Before either of us could block it, the TV landed in the yard and a crack now stretched from one corner of the TV to the other. Even with the police pulling up, Trent was still determined to take the TV, and my determination stood in the TV not moving from its spot. If Trent planned to take it, it would be with my foot through it. The officer now on my lawn seeing what was happening made it clear either we would figure it out or he would take both of us in. Having a record was not what I wanted, so finished with Trent or not, I stormed back into the house leaving the officer and Trent out front.

What had I done? Maybe I shouldn't have looked at Trent's emails. I shouldn't have brought up what I had seen to him. Maybe I was just being insecure. Thought after thought rushed through my mind as I paced the house. I raced to the door only to realize Trent, the *officer, and the TV were now gone. I panicked thinking of being alone once again and ran to grab my cell phone. If I called Trent, he would come back like he had done so many other times. I knew this time was different and not like those times, but he wouldn't just throw all the years away, he couldn't, he wouldn't.*

Trent's phone rang over and over as I held my cell phone up to my ear, but he wasn't answering. Why wasn't he answering my calls? I knew he saw me calling. Was he headed now to be with another woman? Had this been the last straw he needed to permanently drive him back into the arms of his child's mother. I had become used to my mind and thoughts never slowing down, but right now they were in overdrive. I began once again pacing back and forth throughout my living room. My pacing led me outside and had me looking around. Maybe Trent had just pulled down the street, and was trying to figure out what to say, and how to say it to make things better.

Maybe he just needed a breather but he would be right

back. As usual when it came to relationships, I was

wrong. Trent was gone, and the only thing left outside

were the few pieces of shattered glass from the TV.

That was it, I couldn't take it anymore. I was done being

strong. I was done allowing people to hurt me. I was

done letting my guard down and breaking my own rule of

trusting no one. All these years of trying to be strong only

left me still broken and alone. I now had no reason to be

strong with Trent and his boys gone.

Breaking Point

"God, I'm sorry, I can't go on living like this anymore." I was talking out loud as I ran as fast as I could up the flight of stairs leading to my bedroom. I wasn't sure how I was going to end it all, but I knew it had to be tonight. I began searching frantically around my room for anything I could find to aid in the process. I stormed off into my master bathroom and was immediately stopped in my tracks as I stood face to face with myself in the mirror that stretched the length of my whole bathroom. There was no escaping my image and the tears began to flow like never before, only this time the tears weren't for God's help, they were for his forgiveness for what I was about to do. I had cried so many days and to so many mirrors, but today was different. Today would be the last day that I would shed tears in any mirror.

"I tried living this life, God. I prayed many days, and tried leaning on your word, but no matter how much I pray I can't escape this pain, and I feel like you no longer hear me." I wasn't sure if God was even listening now, but time would soon tell.

My phone lay near me as my shaky hands picked it up. I called the one person that I needed to say goodbye to.

"Hey girl," Kindle said, picking up after a couple rings. Hearing her voice for the last time only intensified the tears. Through my cries I told her that I couldn't live like this anymore. I then hit the end button as she was saying something and turned my phone off. I tied a cord around my neck and tried to hang it from my shower rod, but it wasn't strong enough and fell into the shower. I couldn't even end my own life correctly. No matter how hard I tried I failed at everything. I didn't know what I was doing but I was determined to escape the pain, and this time

forever. I tied the cord to the bathroom door, while the other side stayed tightly around my neck and hoped somehow this would do the job of strangling myself, as I pushed the door back. All I managed to do was to suck some of the air out of me. The next thing I vaguely remember were Kindle's cries as she lay beside me, and words from her mouth that weren't registering to my brain.

I was taken by ambulance to a hospital where I was held overnight. I hadn't succeeded in killing myself, nor in making the pain go away, but now for some reason everyone in the hospital wanted to talk to me about why I felt my life was so bad and hard that I needed to end it all. They asked question after question hoping for answers as to why someone "like me" would want to take my life. For years no one asked me these questions. There was no one asking me what it felt like to be in foster care. Nobody, not even the caseworkers thought to ask that one simple question. Are you being treated right? This was never asked but assumed by all that I was. There were no questions asked about how it felt being abandoned by my mother, and then my aunt on two separate occasions. How I felt losing my aunt to cancer. There had never been any questions asked about my well-being, period. If there had been, I may have not been laid up in a hospital bed from a botched attempt to take my own life and once and for all end the racing thoughts and depression.

The doctors and nurses moved quickly around me, acting as if they cared, but they didn't really care or want to know what was really going on inside my head. To protect myself and save time, I told them exactly what they needed to hear to get me out of there. I told them I had a fight with my boyfriend and I wasn't thinking straight. I said that I had never had thoughts of killing myself before, and never would again. They believed every lie I spat out, and planned to release me the next day, but not before prescribing me crazy pills. I knew they didn't really want the truth and I was happy not to give it to them. I also had no plans on taking medication that wouldn't help me. I wasn't crazy.

What should have been a minimum of a three-day stay in the hospital turned into me leaving after only one night. I left the hospital even more broken than when I had arrived. I headed back to the same house, the same issues, and the same demons that refused to go away.

After a failed attempt at suicide, one might think that my next move would be getting some actual help to get better. The day that I decided to act upon ending it all should have been my wake-up call. Instead, it was the continuation of the downward spiral that was my life. I continued to allow my life to collapse all around me. I continued to go to work every day smiling as if nothing had happened. I didn't allow Kindle to bring up what happened, and I would never bring it up myself.

When I got out of the hospital, I just loaded more baggage onto my back and again never sought any help. I lied to myself and to the people around me by pretending that life was okay. I continued convincing myself I wasn't crazy but deep inside, I felt like there was someone trapped inside, begging for someone to truly understand and help her. I didn't want to hurt anymore but was also too embarrassed by my truth. I instead remained quiet.

With Trent gone, I hated how I felt alone in my huge house. I had worked hard for everything I had but I couldn't enjoy it, and honestly wasn't appreciative of any of it. I had started going out and drinking more, hoping it would ease the pain. The drinks and being out with friends made me temporarily forget my problems, but it *was never long before those same unresolved issues came pouring back into my mind, heavier than ever before. The long journey of self-sabotage wasn't coming to an end anytime soon.*

Journey

January 2011, I would continue deeper down my destructive path and put my life in yet another man's hands as I swayed my hips back and forth while out celebrating a friend's birthday. He would whisper in my ear, asking me to dance, and because he was tall and handsome, I would oblige him. He was as smooth as Tennessee Whiskey as he whispered into my ear and had a charm that even surpassed Trent's charm. This chance encounter would change my life forever. I know, I know… meeting in a club should have been the first sign that this was a temporary situation, because up to this point, I hadn't had any luck with men I met in or surrounding nightclubs. I, of course, ignored the red flags because he too spoke the language I wanted to hear. He made all the right moves at a time in my life when I was still waiting for the perfect man to come sweep me out of my slumber. It still hadn't occurred to me, even at almost

30, that being alone and finding myself was what I really needed in life and not a man after all.

In the short time we would take to get to know one another he would change my life forever. I would become pregnant, we would separate, and I would be devastated all within less than a year. With all of the other things that had happened in my life, becoming pregnant and being alone at the age of 30 had never been a concern or thought that ever crossed my mind. All my life I had told myself I would never have kids. I would never bring a child into the world to be depressed and lonely as I had been, but here I was once again changing what I had said. Instead of learning from past experiences, I continued to make the same mistakes over and over. My days and nights were filled with tears wondering how I could make a child happy when I didn't even know how to obtain happiness for myself. I knew better than this situation I had now allowed myself to be in, but was it all a part of a bigger plan?

This chance encounter would be the start of my life changing forever. What God would have in store for me was way greater than anything I could ever imagine, and it would only take three pregnancy tests for me to actually believe it. They would all confirm the exact same thing. I was indeed pregnant, and life once again was about to throw me a curve ball that I wasn't sure I was ready for.

The relationship died like all the others, and I would spend the next 7 to 8 months walking the journey of pregnancy scared and alone. I had friends checking in on me and making sure I got out of the house here and there, but I would never go into detail with them about how going through pregnancy alone only made the depression increase significantly, and the thoughts of death occur even more. Everyone had their issues happening in life, and who would I be to throw my problems at them. I had vowed to myself I would open up more and talk to friends, but this wasn't the time I told myself. My hormones were all over the place and so were my thoughts. How I would add a child to my life of confusion was beyond me. The depression hit me so hard that for a moment I contemplated ending the pregnancy. It was no one but God that helped me see I would be no better than the mom that had given up on me if I aborted my child. I wanted that feeling for no one, especially my own child.

January 30th, 2012 arrived and it was time to head to the hospital to be induced. I had faced many scary moments in life before, but thoughts of feeling not mentally or physically prepared, as well as pushing a little human out of my body, had me shook in a different type of way that was nothing like I had felt before. I knew that I had issues that I would have no choice but to eventually deal with, but I wanted more for my daughter who was about to enter a crazy world that she hadn't asked to come into. I knew I never wanted her to live day to day having to just cope like I had done all my life. I never wanted her suffering day after day and year after year, wondering if her life was even worth living. I had to give her more and I had to heal and live not only for me but now for her as well.

My girlfriends had refused to listen and let me go through labor and delivery alone. My hospital room sat packed to capacity with friends that wouldn't take my usual "I'm good" for an answer. I looked around, realizing that these were all people that I could always rely on. Kindle, who was now married and living in Indianapolis, flew in for a few hours just to be there and fly right back out. If I would have just spoken out before, maybe one of them could have led me in the right direction toward help and healing. I didn't have to hold onto my past alone like I had chosen to do for so long, and my hospital room was proof *of that. From that day on, I knew I had to try harder to communicate with those around me, especially my child.*

After 30 hours of labor, and the dropping heart rate of my baby girl, the doctors decided they had no other choice but to prepare me for an emergency c-section. The thought of natural childbirth had frightened me, but being drugged up more and cut open from one side to the next completely terrified me. Even through the fear, I needed the doctors to do whatever necessary to save my baby. In that very moment, I knew my life would never be just about me again. I was now prepared more than ever to do what my mother hadn't done for me. I would pour the love into her that was never poured into me. I would protect her, unlike how no one protected me. Most importantly I would teach her to seek help if she ever needed it, and to never be ashamed to do so. I would teach her that man was not responsible for her happiness but that it would have to come from within. I would teach her that in her darkest moments she only needed to lean on God.

Thought after thought was rushing through my head as I was being prepared to be transferred from one room to another.

By the time I had been transported to another part of the hospital for my cesarean, I was numb from the waist down. The anesthesiologist sat next to me making small talk as the doctors prepared to cut me open. I didn't need small talk. I needed my daughter and I to survive this procedure. My thoughts drifted to what was happening from my waist down since I could no longer feel anything. How long would it be before I would hear her first cries? Was she okay? Could I become the mother I needed to be for her?

It wasn't long before I heard what I had been waiting on for months. I heard the cry of my sweet angel on earth.

As her dad listened to the nurses and did what they said to cut the umbilical cord, I lay still to get a glimpse of her face. As her cries grew louder, I suddenly found it hard to catch my breath. Panic quickly set in, and thoughts of death instantly flooded my mind.

"I can't breathe." I began to try to turn my head and body to tell the anesthesiologist, but my body wasn't doing what my brain wanted it to do.

"Just try to lay still," the anesthesiologist said. Did he not understand what I was telling him? I once again tried to sit up in hopes my body would cooperate this time and I could get the doctor's attention.

"You have to lay still," the doctor tried telling me. Were they all crazy? The doctor wanted to close me up, the anesthesiologist wanted me to lay still, and I was trying to not die on this metal table. No one was listening to me and my ability to breathe or talk was becoming nonexistent. I couldn't lay still and just stop breathing. My baby needed me.

"I need help," I said, struggling to get it out.

"She can't breathe," I could hear the anesthesiologist finally saying.

"Someone take her," I heard my daughter's father say, handing off our little girl to a nurse. I could hear what was going on all around me but was no longer able to struggle using only my upper body. Lots of feet started scampering into the room, and I could feel bodies all around the room. Something was being put over my face

and mouth but not quick enough for me and my now-shallow breaths that had me scared I wouldn't be around to raise my daughter. I closed my eyes, not knowing my fate but also too exhausted to keep trying to fight for air.

"You gave us a scare," one of the doctors said, standing over me as I opened my eyes. I could tell that whatever had been put over my nose and mouth was now working. It was now easier to breathe and keep my eyes open.

I lay in the recovery room thankful that God had once again chosen to spare my life. I was still in this world for a purpose, but what? Thought after thought rushed through my mind as my hospital room door opened. With all the doctors and nurses rushing in and out of the delivery room to help me, my daughter had been swept out of the room without me getting a good look at her. I prayed it was her so I could finally just hold her and look into her eyes. The nurse walked into my room with my daughter and placed her on my chest. In that very moment I felt a love like I had never known before. An unconditional love that no one would ever be able to take away from us. I would do anything and everything to protect her with all that I had. Seeing her face made me realize that every struggle, broken heart, and disappointment had led me on a journey to this very moment. I looked into the eyes of the child that I would call my daughter and knew she could have no other name than that of Journey.

Point of No Return

By the third day in the hospital, the depression had kicked back in and intensified. I had started crying continuously one day after giving birth to my daughter, and it only continued in the days that followed. I didn't understand why I couldn't stop crying, or why I was even crying at all. The feelings running through me were new ones that I had never experienced before. I shouldn't be sad, I shouldn't feel defeated, I shouldn't feel broken, so why did I? Things were different now. I had a baby girl that needed all of me, and here I was being weak. Through the tears and through the sadness the determination that was hidden so deep down inside me to give my baby girl more than what was ever given to me would have to prevail. I could never allow her to become a motherless child, another statistic of foster care.

I returned home from the hospital depressed and alone. Journey's grandmother had asked if they could take Journey to her house to meet Journey's great grandmother, as well as her father's new girlfriend. It hurt me to say yes, but I was assured it would only be for a few hours at most. I knew I never wanted to come off as bitter, so hesitantly I agreed.

I was dropped off at my front door, after a five day stay in the hospital and almost not making it out alive, only to find mail piled up heavily in my mailbox, and no child in my arms. Even before going into the hospital, I had put off stressing myself over the pile of bills that could care less that I was pregnant and unable to work.

I lay on my couch wondering what my next move would be. The few dollars I had were now gone, and I had fallen behind on my mortgage and car note by months due to my lack of ability to work as much as I had in the past.

My doctor told me that after delivery I needed to be out of work for a minimum of eight weeks, but she had to be crazy if she believed not working was something I could afford to do. My daughter and I would both be sleeping in my car if I didn't get back to work and soon.

Even with returning to work, the streets were still a possibility because I was so far behind on everything that I wasn't sure if I would ever be able to play catch-up. The tears that seemed to come out of nowhere since having my daughter were now streaming harder down my face. I had reached the point of no return in my life. I knew I couldn't return back up my stairs to face that mirror and try once again at succeeding in finally getting rid of the feelings once and forever. I couldn't call on anyone for financial help, and I couldn't return to trying to drink and ignore my feelings away with never-ending house parties and liquor. I couldn't go back to pretending to be living my best life, because pretending wouldn't allow me to provide for my daughter.

I decided instead of laying on the couch crying uncontrollably, I would open my stack of mail—well, at least some of it—and try to figure out life. I flipped through letter after letter before coming across my mortgage statement. I knew I was behind and really didn't need to see another dollar amount owed that I didn't have. I could see through the portion of the letter that was clear that it was not just my regular statement, so I decided "what the hell" and opened it. In it, folded ever-so-nicely was a letter giving me my foreclosure sale date. I knew ignoring all the previous letters from the bank wasn't the best idea, but I was too ashamed to let anyone know what I had gotten myself into.

I dropped to my knees and did what I hadn't done in a very long time. I called out to God like I had never done before.

"God, I am angry. I am angry at myself, but more angry at you. I feel as though you have forsaken me. I no longer come to you because I feel as though you stopped listening to me a long time ago. Maybe you were tired of hearing my cries out to you as I continued putting myself in the same situations over and over again, but I needed you, God. If you could hear me this one last time and not for me, but for Journey, I promise to listen."

The running of my nose and my tears were mixing together, but I didn't care. I was out of breath and hyperventilating at the thought of being homeless with my child. I knew I had been unappreciative of everything that God had blessed me to have, but was I really going to lose everything that I had worked so hard for? In that moment all I could hear was: "I have never left you nor forsaken you. I have been here, my child, waiting for you to get out of your own way." The tears for the moment had stopped, and for the first time in my life, I was listening with open ears and an open heart.

Within four weeks of my c-section, I returned to work, ready to provide the best way I knew how, with hard work. My doctor was skeptical about signing off on my early return to work, since two weeks earlier I had walked into her office and, when asked how I was doing, immediately broke into tears about my mistakes in life, and how I had to do better for Journey. Hesitantly, she told me I had a severe case of postpartum depression that needed to be addressed. All I could do was cry and laugh. One depression wasn't good enough, I now had to deal with another. As my doctor went over all the different medicines to help with depression and anxiety more tears fell. I didn't want to take medicine because I always felt I *could deal, and medicine was for the weak who couldn't handle their issues alone. The doctor assured me that at any time I could choose to stop taking it, but that she wouldn't recommend it. I left my appointment that day and headed to the pharmacy to pick up my prescription for a medicine that I said I would never take. That was the day that my life would once again be changed forever.*

Healing

After a few days of taking medicine, I started to feel like a new person. The crying had stopped, and I felt like I was now ready to take on the world and whatever was to come. I began to sell and give away, piece by piece, the items in my home, not knowing where I was going next. It was as if I was a foster child all over again. Funny thing about this thing called life is how it ends up becoming one complete circle.

I departed the house that I had worked so hard for with nothing but trash bags and hangers of clothing. I didn't even have enough money for boxes by this time. I smiled every day to everyone I knew and told them that I had sold my house and was going to stay in a rental house until I moved to Texas—which had been a dream of mine for as long as I could remember—knowing that with a child and no assistance in Texas, that dream too would wait.

A couple of months later the bank caught up to me and my SUV was repo'd. Of course, that meant the lies continued. I continued lying and told people it had been stolen. I continued to lie to myself, as well as smile and lie to the people around me about what was really going on in my life. Only a couple of friends would ever know my truth until now. That truth that feels so freeing to finally let out.

I made the choice for myself to stop taking my medicine. Something within me knew the depression was gone. I truly believe that feeling was God telling me that he was still with me, and I was going to be okay, that depression no longer had to haunt my mind and body anymore. Two weeks after Journey was born, the sadness, the hurt and pain, all of it was gone. On January 31, 2012, as I lay stretched out, unable to breathe, thinking my daughter was going to be the death of me, she was actually saving me. She had given me a reason to live. She had given me a reason to fight depression like I never had before.

Of course, the devil was in full attack mode and trying to break me, but nothing was going to take me back into that head space that I had yearned to escape for so long. The next few years were beyond rough. Journey and I bounced around from one house to another, depending on person after person to give us rides back and forth and provide a place for us to lay our heads at night. What I hadn't done all my life, I now had no choice but to do. I would have to depend on others in my time of need.

God began opening my heart up once again to His love. It was nothing short of His Grace and mercy that I am here today to tell my story.

If you are wondering where the fairytale ending comes in, let's just say that's for another read. Just know it does come and foster care is definitely not the end of my story, only the beginning.

Forgiveness

My life, like so many others, has been filled with ups and downs. One thing for sure is that every day of sadness that I faced in my past allows me to now find some joy every day that I'm given another chance at life. We are born into this world not knowing what our future holds. We are born only to discover that as sure as we are given breath, one day on our final day, it will leave us forever. I could write and say that because death has encompassed many of my thoughts over the years, and because I believe in God, that I am ready for it whenever it may come, but that would be a lie. What I can say in all honesty is my past and deliverance out of it is what lets me know without a shadow of a doubt that there is a higher power working every day, all around me. Because of this I know that there is a God that sits high and looks low. In those times when I was going through some of my toughest battles that seemed to never end, I did question *if there was really a God. The same God that I questioned when I felt like there was no way I would live to see another day saw enough in me to continuously wake me up day after day. This is why I now choose to be grateful even through the many storms of life.*

Believing that there is a life in Heaven with our Father after this life doesn't mean you won't experience troubles. It also doesn't mean that because you believe in God, riches and wealth are always to physically follow. For me, believing in God means that when you hold onto even that mustard seed grain of faith, He will move mountains that you didn't even know were possible to move.

All my life I prayed to God, even in the moments I doubted him, but it wasn't until recent years that I realized what the problem really was when I thought my prayers were going unheard. I was praying and He was hearing, but it was I who wasn't listening. It took a very long time to understand that when you pray without listening, that's not God not hearing you, that's you not hearing what He is trying to say to you. Today because I actually stop and listen, I am the happiest I have been my whole life. Is it because I'm rich? No! I get up and go to work every day like every other working individual. Am I happy because I face no struggles? Definitely not! I have struggles now more than ever. The difference is, now when I am faced with hard times, I go straight to God in prayer and I LISTEN to what He has to say to me. Is what God has to say to me always what I want to hear? It isn't, but because I now know how to listen, and have experienced firsthand what happens when I don't, every struggle becomes easier to handle, and those storms lighten a lot sooner than before. Today I no longer have to carry that baggage on my back that continuously weighed me down with every step I took.

I now live what I call a simple but happy life because of two beliefs. I believe that there is a God that watches over me and assures me that I am never alone. Secondly, I know that forgiveness is the key. Forgiveness is not for that person but for you and your peace. When you truly forgive people that have hurt you, your mind and heart are healed in a way that changes you from the inside out.

I would see Mrs. Rice on a visit back to Decatur not too long after relocating. We were both sitting eating lunch. I remember seeing her alone in the corner of the empty restaurant. For a brief moment, a feeling of fear was felt. As she ate, she kept her head down, never looking up or even around at her surroundings. Her once strong frame was now even older and in need of assistance from a walker that was placed up against her table. She looked sad as she took bite after bite. At the time I still carried so much anger and hurt towards her that I said nothing, but for some reason I was saddened that she was eating

alone. I couldn't take my eyes off her. Once I had finished

eating, I gave one last glance and left the restaurant. This

would be the last time I would ever see her. Not too long

after that visit, Starsky would call to inform me that she

had passed away. I recall him asking if I was going to go

to the funeral and me wondering why he would even ask

me such a thing. Why would I ever go to her funeral?

This woman had hurt me both physically and mentally

and now she was gone. I thought when the day came

that I would hear she had died, some of the hurt and pain

I felt inside would go away but it didn't. It wasn't until I

forgave her many years later that I was finally able to let

everything from my past with her go. Even though Mrs.

Rice is the name I used for the purposes of this book

only, and you are no longer alive, I forgive you. I now see

that maybe the way you handled me and Starsky was the

only way you knew how. I truly now believe that maybe

you actually thought you were doing your best. Mrs. Rice,

you hurt me and my brother in ways that are never okay, you made a child into a woman when she should have been enjoying just being a kid, but I forgive you. It is because of you that I am the resilient woman I am today, so instead of hanging onto anger, I thank you.

Aunt Wanda, whose name I also changed for the book, I forgive you. You may not truly even know how I feel because like other broken families we have never talked about the past. Still to this day, we have chosen to not acknowledge any past hurt or pain. I used to go home to Decatur from time to time and visit on a holiday and act as if everything was okay. I pretended for many years that the pain you caused was okay. These days I no longer pretend, so the visits have become slim to none year after year. Aunt Wanda, you may have never physically hurt me, but mentally, the damage you caused left me broken about life and family for a very long time. The Bible says that money is the root of all evil, and for our family it definitely was. How you mishandled money that wasn't yours is the reason parts of our family will never be the same again. If you ever read this, know that the money left for me from Aunt Linda that you never planned to give me, I received it. After many months to years that your nephews went back and forth through the courts to get what little money was left, they still felt it in their hearts to give me what Aunt Linda wanted me to have. I don't tell you this to be hurtful or mean. I tell you this in hopes that one day before it's too late you will acknowledge the damage caused to our family by you. I tell you this to let you know that God does heal, and it's never too late to do what is right. On those days when the devil tried to attack my thoughts with reminders of the past, I prayed for both of our peace. Know that I forgive you from the bottom of my heart, and If I hurt you in any way, I also ask that you forgive me.

Mom, as a child I wrote you a long letter asking why, but I will keep my innermost thoughts confined to that letter. From time to time I still wonder why you chose not to raise any of your children, and what happened in your life that led you down the path you took, but those thoughts come way less now that I have found peace within. I realized I got so caught up over the years asking, "Why me, God?" that it took me becoming a mother myself to finally ask, "Why my mother, God?" I now look past my previous pain and can only wonder what it must have felt like for you to give up one child after another. What it must have felt like to watch me and Starsky being taken away that day and how that probably hurt you in a way that you will never forget. I pray that if you have hurt because of the past in any way because of choices you felt were best, or maybe just felt was your only choice at the time, that you have peace. Those of your children that I know and have met are doing just fine. I forgive you, mom.

Lastly, Dovia, I know that you have fought many battles and many demons in your years of life here on earth. I know there have been many times when you put yourself last when you should have been putting yourself first. There were times when your mind, body, and soul suffered because you wanted no one to know the deepest, darkest thoughts of the pain that haunted you day in and out. Because of this, you fell deeper and deeper into despair, never seeking the help that you severely needed. You tried to take care of those all around you, but you always forgot to take care of the little girl glaring in the mirror back at you.

Most of your life has been spent straying away from your past instead of embracing what has made you the woman you are today. When you raise your voice to Journey, you beat yourself up for days, wondering if you are not being the best mom you can be. Dovia, it is okay.

You are giving her the life and love that you never had, and that alone will stay with her forever. I forgive you, Dovia. I was always waiting for you to find that inner peace that has always been within you, and you finally did. Keep living and breathing life into yourself and others, because that is your divine purpose and the reason you are here. "Forgiveness is Love, and Love is Life, and God is in the center of it all."

P.S. I'm not sure what God has for me in my next journey in life, but I am ready for it. Being a survivor of foster care means I have no choice.

A poem for you

This authenticity, this moving forward, this pushing; it hurts like hell. It hurts because my strength is so weak making every little thing painful. It is like being hit with all the hardships of life over and over again and my body already covered in bruises. It is living in a constant war with hope and fate. It is living with another war, peace and acceptance. It is living with yet again, another war with accepting love and feeling undeserving of any kind of love. It is wanting your help, but not wanting to need anyone. It is living with war after war in my head, but right now, all at once. It is just begging for the world to be gentle with my storm-raging soul. I don't know what I'm doing 100 percent of the time. I live in constant exhaustion. When I have a chance to laugh, I do it so hard, and for a moment I feel a little less numb, but only for a second. Any amount of joy gets counted at the end of the day, and it's enough to keep me sane, and lead me *to taking deep breaths, and press on to the next day. I*

am not sure if authenticity is the answer, or if it just keeps

me alive, but it's working right now, and if my hell helps

you, then that's what I'll do.

I know I'll see this through. My joy will not only not hold

any weight, it will in fact release the weight I'm carrying

right now. I'm heavy with many things right now. But my

walls are falling, and I'm afraid, but not alone.

My faith is something that I cannot lose, but right now my

heart is faint, and I'm doing my best to praise God for the

moments that I have relief. So if you know me, and you

see me struggling, but notice good things (any good

things), tell me, because sometimes I don't see the

reasons I need to praise God. He is worthy of more

praise than I give. After all, He is the reason I see any

good at all

~Morgan Bassett

Thank you, Morgan, for allowing me to share what so many feel, but can't put into words as you have... There is a rainbow at the end of the storm ♡